THRIVE in the Future of Work is a ticket to a tra~~r~~
you have to do is read it, do what Kevin recomme~~nds and find yourself~~
free to define your own life and work, no longer an underpaid slave to a
distant boss but master of your own life and destiny. This book should
be read by everybody (especially everyone under 50) interested in
shaping the future world of work for themselves and others. It will
change their lives and ultimately change the world we live in. It is *that*
important.

> **Charles Handy**, best-selling author of *The Empty Raincoat* and *The Elephant and the Flea*

When I sat down to read Kevin's draft copy of **THRIVE in the Future of Work**, I was swamped with work and the last thing I needed was another book to add to the pile on my bedside table. But I could not stop reading! Thank you, Kevin, for writing this amazing easy-to-read book that summarizes so many important Future of Work concepts at both individual and organizational level. This book is a gem for anybody who is curious about the agile mindset and wants to understand how fundamental it is for adapting to the changing world of work. Read it to understand what agility looks like – and ultimately to thrive in the Future of Work.

> **Pia-Maria Thorén**, Founder and Inspiration Director, Agile People

This is a wonderful book that provides a clear and practical roadmap on how to embed agility into the systems and DNA of an organization, as well as in the mindsets of individuals. It will be an invaluable resource for the boardroom and the HR department, as well as for individuals and leaders. Don't just buy this book, read it!

> **Costas Markides**, Professor, Strategy and Entrepreneurship / Holder, Robert Bauman Chair in Strategic Leadership, London Business School

In a space dominated by general trends, sound bites and predictions about the world of work, **THRIVE in the Future of Work** puts the individual at the center of the debate.

> **Tracy Dodd**, Head of Global Talent, Tiffany & Co.

Navigating a world of work that is in a constant state of flux is a critical challenge for organizations and individuals alike. In **THRIVE in the Future of Work**, Kevin Empey charts a path through the complexity with an ambition not only to navigate these challenges but to help individuals to thrive in the new world of work. The book is packed with practical insights for leaders and employees to lead themselves and their organizations in the exciting and precarious times we find ourselves in. It is essential reading for anyone with the ambition to take ownership of the Future of Work for their individual career and/or their organizational strategy.

> **David Collings**, Professor of Human Resource Management, Dublin City University

The Future of Work is not only about "work;" it is also about our human condition and our society as a whole. Kevin addresses this elegantly in this highly informative book and provides hugely valuable insight for anyone rethinking their strategy and wishing to be prepared for that future.

    John Herlihy, ex-VP Google and ex-VP EMEA & LATAM, LinkedIn

Kevin Empey has done a masterful job of folding the future into the present in one of the most prevalent settings in life: our work and working life. By focusing on the rapidly-changing nature of the Future of Work, Kevin builds a compelling case for embracing agility for the uncertain and changing business world. With the logic, insights, tools, and examples contained in this book, mastering agility will turn threat and uncertainty into future opportunity and daily practice. Bravo!

    Dave Ulrich, Rensis Likert Professor of Business, Ross School of Business / Partner, The RBL Group

THRIVE in the Future of Work is an essential primer on the "irrefutable realities" facing us as business leaders of the post-pandemic era. Kevin Empey provides evidence and actionable roadmaps to sense, proactively respond to and lead the ongoing change coming at us with increased frequency in the modern age. Throughout, Kevin offers tools and techniques for what we can do to be a pro-active shaper of our organizational and individual working lives.

    Kevin Mulcahy, Co-Author, *The Future Workplace Experience*

There are times as senior leaders when we need to get out of the weeds and look around us to see and appreciate what is happening, particularly in times of rapid change and great uncertainty. To have Kevin's thinking as a guide, and as a source of good practical advice and insight, will really help us understand the context in which we must operate and the tools and skills necessary to not just survive but to thrive.

    David Cagney, Chief Human Resources Officer, Irish Civil Service

In tackling the practical realities and implications of the Future of Work, Kevin Empey's book demystifies the skills needed for business and personal agility which are such critical and strategic topics across industry today.

    James O'Connor, VP, Microsoft International Operations

The Future of Work is here – and ready for the taking. Kevin takes readers on an eye-opening and most fascinating journey into the challenging yet inevitable and rewarding world of agility. This is a book is full of important information for those brave enough to shape and thrive in the new world of work.

    Fabiola Eyholzer, Co-Founder, Just Leading Solutions

For years, Kevin Empey has been at the forefront of the Future of Work topic. As always, his analysis is distinguished by a refreshing focus on practicality: exploring the reality of how organizations and working lives are changing today and tomorrow ... and what leaders must do to get ahead of, and navigate, these trends. In **THRIVE in the Future of Work**, Kevin provides an invaluable blueprint that enables us all to make sense of changes that are already all around us and to hone our agility for the journey ahead.

    Simon Boucher, Chief Executive Officer, Irish Management Institute

THRIVE in the Future of Work is a joy to read, with every page giving practical and accessible accounts and tips for leaders, for HR and for individuals to navigate the changing world of work, in the most engaging way. What's particularly impressive is how this book inspires you to think from different perspectives on an organizational level but layers on what you, as an individual, can do to thrive. This isn't an ordinary business book, it's a powerful, engaging and inspiring piece of work, that will keep you thinking long after you put it down.

    Aisling Teillard, Co-Founder and CEO at Our Tandem

Kevin Empey is a leader in the Future of Work debate and this book again takes his work to the international stage. **THRIVE in the Future of Work** combines both academic research and practitioner insight in a highly readable way. The need for personal agility to thrive in the new world of work is clearly presented and the book is full of practical advice on how to prepare for the future world of work. His recommendations on how to master personal and organizational agility will find a receptive audience amongst employees and leaders, while the lessons distilled for leadership development will resonate with HR practitioners internationally. I strongly recommend this book.

    Patrick Flood, Professor of Organizational Behavior, Dublin City University Business School

Any leader who wants to be more successful must read Kevin's book. After 40 years as a leader in the military, business and public sector, much of it developing senior leaders, it's clear to me that agility is one of the top three drivers of success. In a dynamic world, the other drivers – effective task delivery and engaging people – are themselves dependent on agility to optimize them to the environment. Agility as a deliberate and core capability has been neglected for far too long in the development of all but military leaders. Kevin shows agility is not some mystical gift you are born with, giving every reader the opportunity to truly understand, develop and deliver agility to become more successful and future-fit. Buy it, read it, do it!

    Chris Roebuck, Hon. Visiting Professor of Transformational Leadership, Cass Business School

Kevin's stimulating book, full of insights and practical advice, is a thought-provoking invitation for business leaders and HR professionals to embark on a purposeful learning journey towards enterprise agility: start now, and start small; find your "buddy group;" get the right talents; and, together, let us all ensure we will truly thrive, rather than just survive, in the Future of Work! A really great read.

Otti Vogt, COO and Chief Transformation Officer C&G, ING

The world of work is changing rapidly. Kevin's book skillfully navigates us through the practical implications of these changes and how we can thrive in the future. ***THRIVE in the Future of Work*** contains a powerful blend of facts, research, case studies and tools, all underpinned by a clear focus on acting with purpose and agility. This is an important read for all of us in business and in the people profession.

Peter Cheese, Chief Executive, Chartered Institute of Personnel & Development (CIPD)

As events in recent years have proven, the uncertain nature of our future is one of the only certain things in life. What Kevin has so eloquently brought to life in his book is the understanding that, for all of us, the Future of Work is essentially about agility and how we build agility into our organizational and individual lives.

Evan Leybourn, Co-Founder and CEO, Business Agility Institute

With a rare gift of simplicity and common-sense in an overcooked library of complexity, mumbo-jumbo and clichés, Kevin has brought the possibility of our working tomorrows into our today in the most relatable and consumable way. A must-have for everyone with leadership ambitions and curious about the realities of the Future of Work.

Ger Mitchell, CHRO and Corporate Development Director, Permanent tsb

To start with the conclusion: if you believe that the Future of Work will be not the same as it is today, read this book. Why? Because Kevin's roadmap will definitely help, his insights are provoking, his many case studies are inspiring. However, I hope you will not only read the book, but actually start doing, start implementing what's inside. Start your journey, shape your future! Your people deserve it, your organization deserves it, you and your family deserve it! Let's change work for good!

Tom Van der Lubbe, Co-Founder, Viisi Mortgages

THRIVE in the Future of Work is a pragmatic and insightful book that will help any leader adjust to the new workplace paradigm with confidence. This is a no-nonsense guide for leaders charged with shaping the next phase of work and working life for the workplaces of today and tomorrow.

Dan Schawbel, *New York Times* best-selling author and Managing Partner, Workplace Intelligence

Kevin's book offers a hands-on approach and guide to the Future of Work. He helps us on a practical journey towards greater agility, guiding readers through the essential need for personal agility and then exploring the roles of Leaders and HR in enabling organizational agility. Kevin also importantly touches on the societal imperatives for the Future of Work so that no one is left behind in the emerging and ever-changing work environment. The book offers plenty of fresh ideas and tools so that you are equipped for this journey – after all, you cannot solve tomorrow's problems with yesterday's thinking.

    Mihaly Nagy, Founder and CEO, The HR Congress Summit Series

In 2020, organizations globally were catapulted into a virtual world. Today, organizations need to reshape work and the workplace – to allow both the individual and the organization to continue to thrive and adapt. Kevin's book, an insightful and practical guide, will help both organizations and the individuals who lead and work in them to take on learnings from recent years, to help shape a new and better world of work for the individual, the organization and society. A highly valuable and timely book.

    Julie Sinnamon, CEO, Enterprise Ireland

THRIVE in the Future of Work offers a combination of strategic models, use cases and industry research to challenge leaders at all levels to rapidly adapt and not simply react to the multitude of competing requirements. HR has an opportunity to act strategically and to create a more integrated, agile and self-sustaining system of personal and organizational engagement. As individuals and organizations navigate the complexity of new ways of working, Kevin Empey offers clear and actionable guidance to create skill sets and mindsets essential for the Future of Work.

    Amy Loomis, Ph.D., Research Director, Future of Work, IDC

This is a great book that systematically details how to create future ready teams and individuals. Kevin's holistic view, covering both outside-in and inside-out approaches to rethinking organization structure, skills, and culture, helps us all to move forward in the uncertain, post-COVID Fourth Industrial Revolution.

    Shu-Tze, Author of *Human Race 4.0: The Science of Getting Ahead in the New World Order*

By bringing his talents to unpack concepts associated with the Future of Work, Kevin has produced an essential text for our time. **THRIVE in the Future of Work** combines compelling evidence, practical guidance and a genuine empathy and kindness for everyone seeking to carve out routes to success amidst shifting organizational landscapes.

    Dr. Jean Cushen, Associate Professor of HRM, Maynooth University School of Business

There's nothing quite like a global pandemic to underscore the value of agility. Kevin's book has arrived *just-in-time* for the next phase of adaptation in the world of work. His practical guidance helps readers make tangible steps forward as we reimagine how work will evolve for years to come. Kevin strikes a healthy balance between what is good for the individual and for the organization, as both need each other. The principles he outlines are evergreen but are put in today's context – fostering a growth mindset in our ability to learn, adapt and thrive in an environment that will remain ever-changing.

Mary Slaughter, Global Head of Employee Experience, Morningstar, Inc.

The Future of Work has approached all of us at a much faster pace than we expected. Individuals, teams, and organizations need to be agile to not only cope with the challenges but also to thrive during the uncertain and challenging times ahead. If you are looking for answers to what, when and how we work and live better in the present and future, this book is for you.

Na Fu, Associate Professor Trinity Business School and Digital Workplace Lead, Trinity Centre for Digital Business

As organizations struggle to tackle new sources of competitive disruption that challenge both customer and colleague retention, C-suite execs should reach for this pragmatic playbook on how to best navigate the challenges of today and tomorrow. Kevin Empey's deftly written book demystifies the Future of Work and provides an easy-to-follow guide that will benefit leaders of organizations big and small as they chart the course to continued success.

Susan Steele, Chief HR Officer, Ocean Technologies Group, and Advisory Board Member, Open Classrooms London

THRIVE

IN THE

FUTURE OF WORK

*How Embracing an Agile Mindset Will
Benefit You and Your Organization*

Kevin Empey

Published by Oak Tree Press, Cork, Ireland

www.oaktreepress.com / www.SuccessStore.com

© 2021 Kevin Empey

A catalogue record of this book is available from the British Library.

ISBN 978 1 78119 455 3 (paperback)
ISBN 978 1 78119 456 0 (ePub)
ISBN 978 1 78119 457 7 (Kindle)
ISBN 978 1 78119 458 4 (PDF)

Cover design: George B. Stevens, G Sharp Design.

Graphics: Wesley Strickland.

CONTENTS

FIGURES

TABLES

CASE EXAMPLES

To Brona, to whom I owe so much already. Your patience and support has been incalculable.

To Conor, Alistair and Marcus, thank you for your continued tolerance and for the daily gift of you just being you.

To Walton and Louie: your lives and example have provided me with the conscience, curiosity and concern to ask questions such as those raised in this book.

ACKNOWLEDGEMENTS

I am deeply indebted and grateful to countless people and contributors whose work, support, and ideas are the real sources of the content in this book.

I would particularly like to acknowledge the writings and thought leadership of those who take the time to help us all to think about and shape the "Future of Work." Their work and words encourage us to think about the opportunities and choices we have as a society, as organizations and as individuals. They challenge us to take advantage of advances in technology, new ways of working and progressing human potential, while also ensuring that such advancement benefits us all and does not result in some being left behind. Of the many such gifted writers and contributors, special appreciation goes to Dave Ulrich and Charles Handy whose pioneering work over the years has continuously prompted my own curiosity into where the world of work is going and why. From more recent times, sincere thanks to Kevin Mulcahy for his ongoing support, insight and expertise in this field.

Thank you also to the many business and HR leaders who took the time from their day to allow me to interview them for this book – their lived experience, insight and leadership at the sharp and practical end of shaping the Future of Work has been invaluable.

To Dr. Jean Cushen, who was always there to support and challenge my ideas and how they were presented.

To Brooke White, who has been such a valued partner through the writing process but also through her constant and continuous encouragement.

And to Brian O'Kane, of Oak Tree Press, who answered my call at the beginning and fragile stage of this journey and stuck with me all the way.

FOREWORD

The past shapes today's public actions and private reflections. But the past is past. The future offers opportunities for what can be: envisioning ambitions yet to be realized, embracing optimism about possibilities, and ensuring confidence that today's actions may lead to tomorrow's good fortune. Folding future aspirations into today's practical actions helps all of us learn from, and not be constrained by, our past.

Kevin Empey has done a masterful job of helping fold the future into the present in one of the most prevalent settings in life: our work and working life. Most of us spend an inordinate amount of time thinking about and doing work. Where, how, and what work we do defines our role, shapes our identity, and often determines our well-being. And now, probably more than at any time in our history, the assumptions about how and where we work are being revisited all over the world.

By focusing on the rapidly changing nature of the Future of Work, Kevin helps each of us envision ambitions, embrace possibilities, and ensure confidence so that we can realize our full potential.

In this book, Kevin helps us imagine and chart our better future by taking us through a simple, but profound and compelling, logic structure.

Step 1: *The future is uncertain*

Given the multiple disruptions and crises of recent times (global pandemic, civic unrest, political divisiveness, economic volatility, and emotional *malaise*), no one can predict a new normal. Instead of offering false hope by defining an unknowable "new normal" or giving up hope by tolerating uncertainty, it is important to learn how to harness uncertainty, which means to have realistic optimism about what might happen, to use uncertainty as an inflection point for reinvention, and to proactively create a positive future.

Step 2: *Harnessing uncertainty requires agility*

In a world where we neither anticipate nor control the change context, we have to rely on our ability to harness uncertainty. Agility becomes both the individual competence and organizational capability to discover opportunity from uncertainty. Drawing on a vast literature about change, flexibility, transformation, innovation, learning, creativity, and resilience, agility may be defined around four dimensions:

- Create a future;
- Anticipate opportunity;
- Respond quickly; and
- Learn always.

By understanding and mastering these four facets of agility, uncertainty may be harnessed and a positive future created. Kevin's work translates these facets and dimensions of agility in workable and practical ways that can be applied to our personal and working lives.

Step 3: Agility may be demonstrated in multiple settings

As Kevin's book outlines in eloquent detail, these four dimensions of agility show up in four settings: strategy; organization; leader; and individual.

Strategic agility differentiates winning business strategies as they pivot from:

- Industry expert to industry leader;
- Market share to market opportunity;
- Who we are to how customers respond to us;
- Penetrating existing markets to creating new and uncontested markets;
- Beating competition to redefining competition.

Strategic agility is less about what an organization does to win now and more about how to build a capacity for continual strategic change. It means continually and rapidly updating choices about where to play and how to win.

Organizational and team agility enables the organization to anticipate and rapidly respond to dynamic market conditions. Organizations and teams that cannot change as fast as their external demands quickly fall behind, never catching up. Rapid response to future customer opportunities and fast innovation of products, services, and business models differentiate organizations that win. Organizational agility is enhanced when organizations:

- Create autonomous market-focused teams that can move rapidly to create and define new opportunities;
- Allow values to evolve to match the desired culture and firm identity; and
- Discipline themselves to make change happen fast.

These organizations continually experiment, improve, remove boundaries inside between silos and outside with customers, and create networks or ecosystems for improvement.

Leadership agility becomes a core differentiating competence of effective leaders at all levels and across industries. High potential leaders can be identified based on their learning agility, which can be defined, assessed, and improved to create a leadership pipeline. Learning leaders seek opportunities in what can be more than rehashing the past, in creating more than replicating, and in inspiring others to be their best selves. Leadership agility comes in part from predisposition (nature and DNA), which are part of an individual's neurology, and implies hiring individuals who are naturally agile (learn, change, and act quickly). But learning agility also can be enhanced through training on asking questions, taking risks, experimenting with new ideas and actions, continuously improving by auditing what worked and what did not, observing others, being resilient, embarking on stretch assignments, receiving feedback, and so forth.

Ultimately, as Kevin clearly explains, agility comes from within us all as individuals and our mindset about the choices we make about the future. **Individual agility** is the ability of people to learn and grow. Agile individuals are open, find personal well-being and deliver better business results. Individual learning agility is the competence of an employee to learn and grow as a leader or an employee and is the basis of talent management today. Individuals who cannot change as fast as their work and environment demands will struggle to adapt as the rapidly changing world of work unfolds. Kevin's work is a masterclass in helping us to understand and apply the concept of personal agility to our work and working lives. He demonstrates how personal agility is both a mindset (growth mindset, curiosity) and a set of skills (asking questions, taking appropriate risks). Individual learning agility applies not just in work settings, but in most areas of our lives … family, community, hobbies, and day-to-day living.

Step 4: Human resource work enables and institutionalizes agility

HR practices around people, performance, information, and work can be crafted to foster and enable strategic, organization, leadership, and individual agility. People can be hired, promoted, and trained to signal and encourage organizational and personal agility. Rewards can be aligned to agility or to the ability to change and adapt. Information can be shared about successful change efforts to illustrate both successful and unsuccessful change. Finally, work can be organized to foster agility.

These four steps shape the logic in this exceptional book. Kevin builds the case for agility in the uncertain and changing current business world. He helps us all as individuals to recognize and create an agile mindset along with specific skills to do so. From the basis of mindset being at the heart of our decision-making for the Future of Work, he explores organization systems that instill agility. He reviews how leaders model agility. And he suggests specific ways HR can enable and institutionalize agility. *Bravo!*

With the logic, insights, tools, and examples contained in this book, mastering agility will turn threat and uncertainty into opportunity and daily practice.

Dave Ulrich
Rensis Likert Professor of Business, Ross School of Business
Partner, The RBL Group
Alpine, Utah

Introduction

AN INVITATION

The future is not inevitable. We can influence it,
if we know what we want it to be.

Charles Handy

I have never been a huge fan of the term "Future of Work," though it feels like it is everywhere these days. With no literal meaning to speak of, it is simply a convenient label that tries to encompasses multiple topics impacting the world of work today. It is a universal expression that refers to the profound trends and changes impacting work and working life, driven by forces ranging from exponential digitalization and globalization, to societal changes, robotics, artificial intelligence, shifts in consumer behavior, and remote working. At the heart of this book is the challenge that Charles Handy's quote presents to us all about this future. We explore how these Future of Work forces and developments *really* impact us as individuals and as organizations in practical terms. How, for example, can we learn to navigate and thrive in a world of work that is changing so fast? And for those of us who have a role in shaping the Future of Work for our organizations, our workforces, and for wider society, how can we ensure that we are making work better and making work matter for others?

History tells us that every significant revolution in how and where we work has always been triggered by a step change in technology: consider the wheel, the steam engine, the computer, and the Internet. Moore's Law of Computing states that the technological power and changes in the modern era we now live in are exponential and compounding rather than simply incremental or linear, and so we can expect changes in how and where work is done ultimately to be just as profound.

Work needs to be designed to build better societies, not just better organizations and more efficient economies.

Every week we hear new reports about how the world of work is changing. Many believe we are going through the biggest change to working life since the Industrial Revolution. Driven by advances in technology, global inter-connectedness, and the emergence of a multi-generational workforce with different expectations regarding work and the workplace, new disruptors and innovations are appearing across every aspect of working life. But amongst the continuous noise, somehow, life goes on. The sun rises just as it did yesterday. And for many, before COVID-19 at least, the busy demands, rituals, and routines of work seem to remain relatively unchanged.

So, when will this new revolution, or the Future of Work, really hit us? Has COVID-19 provided the circuit-breaking global experience that will prompt a step change in the assumptions we have created for ourselves about what, where, when, how, and by whom work will be done in the future? Or will we return to familiar patterns of behavior, only to be disrupted by the next change to our organizations or economies? When (if ever) will the hype around the so-called Future of Work become yesterday's news?

The world of work has always undergone change. As humans, haven't we constantly adapted and evolved from one cycle to the next? Isn't it just what we do? Perhaps, for some, like the unfortunate frog in a gradually heating pot of water, the change may feel incremental but profound to the point where all has changed utterly around us. And so it is perhaps with organizations and working life.

The significant difference in this, our current phase, is the sheer pace and frequency of change combined with the variety of *converging* forces and rapidly evolving technologies hitting us at the same time. It's a climate change meets aging population meets global connectivity meets self-driving cars sort of thing!

We are now experiencing a digital world that is gradually replacing a more traditional or "analog" world, with its deeply rooted assumptions, norms, and mindsets regarding work, careers, and organizational life. Changes will be required as to how we individually and collectively approach this new phase. But surely it is also true to say that many fundamental human traits and leadership characteristics will remain as important and enduring as ever?

A fundamental shift is underway

While robots, automation, and millennials perhaps grab all the headlines, it is a fact that a fundamental shift is happening in the world of work. Policy-makers, organizations, and individuals need to take notice of this shift now and deal with it proactively rather than find themselves in catch-up mode. This shift offers great promise, opportunity, and human benefit, but also potential risk and downsides in the form of underemployment, inequity, and the devaluation of work.

The precise nature of the changes we are seeing in areas such as jobs and organizational design are difficult to predict. But declining levels in engagement and organizational trust, coupled with increasing levels of precarious work, workplace stress, and widening pay gaps are just some of the clear warning signs that we have some tough choices ahead, especially if the goal is to create broad-based prosperity and sustainable work models for all people in the future.

The decisions we make today regarding organizational design, jobs, and careers will shape the world of work in the future. The following questions are amongst those that we need to consider:

- What are the practical implications of this new world of work for:
  o *Individuals*, who need to future-proof their careers and working lives?
  o *Business leaders*, who are building the organizations of tomorrow?
  o *People and HR leaders*, who have a key role to play in shaping the Future of Work?
  o *Organization*s as a whole?
- What do these implications tell us about the wider ethical and policy requirements from society and governments in how work/labor policy, education, skills development, social security, and taxation are approached?

This book explores these questions and provides practical suggestions, research, and case studies to help the reader take their own steps into the Future of Work with confidence, optimism, and purpose. The intention is to foster greater awareness of the skillsets and mindset needed to thrive, rather than just survive, in the changing but exciting future that lies ahead. Consider this book as an *invitation* to stop and engage in a constructive conversation about how we can individually, collectively, and proactively shape the new world of work.

I recall my father telling me a story when he was in his mid-career years. He was thinking through about his future, the challenges he was facing at that time, what actions to take next, and so on. While out walking one day with all this complexity racing in his mind, he passed a sign that quoted the old saying: "Don't just do something, sit there." The simplicity of the invitation and message stopped him in his tracks. The phrase was adapted, I understand, from the actor, Martin Gabel, back in the 1940s. My father did indeed pause and heed that advice, and set about de-cluttering his mind, focusing on the facts and what he could control. He found his path forward, which allowed him to move on and, with Louie his partner in life, to continue an outstanding life of service to countless people they met from every walk of life.

> **The concept and practices associated with agility are necessary to be Future of Work ready.**

His story reminds me of where we have all perhaps been in recent years when it comes to the Future of Work topic. There's so much noise and clutter about the Future of Work, and we're caught up in the futile rush to somehow keep up with and control everything going on. Perhaps, instead, we should take a moment to just stop: to reflect on where we are and what is really happening around us and inside of us so that we can move forward with purpose, abundance and confidence. I hope this book helps you in some small way with that pursuit.

So, what does the Future of Work mean for me?

While we might accept there are some fundamental changes happening in the world of work, we are still left with the question: What does it all mean for me? Not in conceptual terms, but for me now, today, next week, or next year? What needs to change, and what needs to say the same?

THRIVE in the Future of Work tackles these questions and tries to reduce the clamor of information around the topic. It explores what individual leaders and employees can do in practical terms to lead their organizations and themselves through this exciting but precarious time. Throughout the book, we will explore both the practical and personal realities (as well as the implications) of the changing world of work for individuals, business leaders, and HR leaders.

With a particular focus on the individual, this book suggests that the concept and practices associated with agility are necessary to be Future of Work ready. Simply put, if we could all shift our skillset and mindset from a traditional approach to work to a more "agile" way of doing things – on both individual and organizational levels – we would go a long way toward being prepared to navigate whatever disruption (technological, medical, economic, and otherwise) inevitably lies ahead.

Over the past 30 years, I've been an active participant in and observer of the changing world of work. I have been lucky to work in a diversity of domains ranging from economic and leadership development, to technology, HR strategy, and employment policy. A common theme throughout my career has been helping organizations to create engaging, sustainable and rewarding work environments and helping people stay in touch with the factors associated with the changing world of work and employment. I've also had the privilege of researching and working with many amazing people and organizations that truly exemplify a Future of Work mindset. These pages contain their work, their stories and their combined experiences to help you create your own Future of Work.

The structure of this book

THRIVE in the Future of Work has four distinct parts:

- **Part One: The Changing World of Work**
  - o *Chapter 1: The Future of Work* summarizes the shifts and trends apparent in the world of work and how they have intensified in recent years;
  - o *Chapter 2: The Case for Agility* examines the concept of agility and outlines its impact on organizations, the world of work, and individual careers;
- **Part Two: Personal Agility**
  - o *Chapter 3: The Agile Mindset* argues that Future of Work readiness requires all individuals – employees, employers, business leaders, and HR professionals – to adopt a mental, learning attitude or mindset that is positively oriented toward constant change, complexity, and uncertainty;
  - o *Chapter 4: The Agile Skillset* introduces a research-based Personal Agility Model, detailing the necessary individual skills and behaviors for agility and to be able to successfully navigate the challenges and opportunities that will continue to emerge from the changing work environment;
- **Part Three: Shaping the Future Ready Organization**
  - o *Chapter 5: A New Employment Deal for the Future of Work* addresses the Future of Work challenge and opportunity for both employers and individuals. Contrasting these with the experiences of previous generations, we introduce the case for a "New Deal" between employees and employers that reflects the impending realities of the Future of Work;

- o *Chapter 6: Future Ready Leaders* provides an overview of what has changed for leaders over recent times and addresses the practical leadership skills they need for the new challenges they face tomorrow and beyond;

- o *Chapter 7: Future Ready HR* explores the history of the HR function and where it has come from, before examining the unique role the HR leader and function can play in shaping the Future of Work. This chapter will also help those who need to identify, hire, develop, and retain people with the skills of the future, and to create an environment for them to thrive;

- o *Chapter 8: Organizational Agility – A System Perspective* presents an approach and a toolkit to generate greater understanding of an organization's current agility and what can be done to progress a pathway towards improved organizational agility.

- **Part Four: A Call to Action for the Future**

- o *Chapter 9: Societal Implications for the Future of Work* broadly examines the emerging choices for navigating the Future of Work at the societal level, especially in relation to areas such as education and employment policy. We explore what is needed from all of us as a society to proactively create an environment for broad-based prosperity and for "good work" to thrive into the future;

- o *Chapter 10: Your Call to Action in Shaping the future of Work* summarizes the key messages from the book and outlines five practical steps you can take in navigating your own path into the Future of Work.

Inside these pages, you will find:

- A look at the facts and illustrations of the key points;
- Practical stories and examples from those who have embraced Future of Work challenges and opportunities;
- Forward-looking guidance and recommendations for your context, and how to move forward with confidence and skill; and
- Practical considerations, questions, and exercises to help you on the road ahead.

Also, throughout the book, we highlight several case studies of well-known and some less-known organizations that have already embraced agility, a Future of Work mindset as well as specific processes that support individual growth, and a new type of employment deal for their workforce. We are not saying that everything these organizations do is perfect, but we highlight their work as examples of how they have shown leadership and courage in shaping the Future of Work with new and vibrant ideas, structures and processes that we can all learn from.

Embracing tomorrow's potential

There's an ancient Danish proverb, later attributed to Niels Bohr and others, that says:

> *Prediction is very difficult, especially when the future is concerned.*

It sums up the peril of trying to predict what the future will hold with. Nobody knows precisely where this Future of Work will take us. It's a bit like Columbus setting out on his quest without a detailed map. Columbus and his crew may not have known what lay ahead but they had an ultimate goal, ambition and purpose, adaptability, resilience, and skill – qualities we can learn from –

that sustained them throughout their voyage and many varied discoveries.

What if we could develop the adaptive qualities and mindset, not just to sustain ourselves though the next phase of work but to thrive and positively engage with it? Work is too important to simply be endured or coped with. We need to fully embrace it and its importance as a meaningful part of our lives. Work needs to be designed to build better societies not just better organizations and more efficient economies. Surely, the human race – so brilliant in its ingenuity and proven ability to adapt – can create a future that offers broad-based security and prosperity for all its citizens.

This book offers a wider story than just individual and organizational Future of Work resilience and readiness. It is a request to embrace and take part in a wider societal challenge to create a Future of Work that is of value and of benefit to all – to ensure that no one is left behind.

Part One

THE CHANGING WORLD OF WORK

Chapter 1
THE FUTURE OF WORK

The future is already here – it's just not very evenly distributed.

William Gibson

In the late 16th century, Queen Elizabeth I refused a patent for a ground-breaking automated knitting machine. Her fear was that it would take away income potential from the laborers, who "obtain their daily bread by knitting." New ways of working have always provoked contrasting perspectives and opinions. Emotions tend to range from concern and even fear of the unknown, to excitement and optimism for a better future.

Before and since the Industrial Revolution, the way in which work is organized and executed has been continuously changing and evolving. Yet, the digitally empowered period we are entering – commonly referred to as the "Future of Work" – is seeing as fundamental a transformation of working life as the Industrial Age itself.

The topic has received considerable attention from academia, commentators, and industry leaders in recent years. There are others, however, who suggest the organizational and individual consequences and challenges we face today are not necessarily all that dramatic or new; we are simply following a natural evolutionary trend. While the pandemic no doubt has accelerated our assumptions about where, when, and how work is done, such developments and trends were already well underway before then.

Over 30 years ago, management thought leader Charles Handy used the term "shamrock organization" to describe the fragmented nature of emerging organizational and work design. Essentially, he described organizations as ecosystems made up of various suppliers and individual contributors that deliver products and services, rather than a single, fixed all-encompassing entity. Handy accurately predicted the blend of permanent, contracted, and agency work necessary to deliver the variety of products and services in the modern organization at optimum cost. There are myriad examples of how trends, such as contingent working and organizational agility, have been seen before. Many argue that, in a constant quest for what is new and trendy, we fail to appreciate the lessons and enduring legacies from previous cycles in the world of work.

For example, the current hot topic of the "gig economy," which describes temporary, flexible jobs *versus* full-time employment, is not a new phenomenon. In the 1700s and in centuries prior, the dominant means of earning income was through cottage industries or as artisans, tradesmen, and seasonal workers. Today, while figures vary around the globe, more than a quarter of the workforce participates in the gig economy in some capacity, and more than one in 10 workers relies on gig work for their primary income. The debate about new ways of doing work and its impact on jobs goes back even further, as Queen Elizabeth's intervention in the knitting industry demonstrates.

It is true, however, that we are now moving into a more technologically enabled, fast changing and distributed phase of work and working life than ever before. This phase will cause a material and significant disruption to how we live and work, just as previous technological advancements – the steam engine, electrical power, and the computer (see **Figure 1.1**) – triggered previous revolutions. This new period of exponential advancement lays the case that we are indeed in the Fourth Industrial Revolution, with all the attention and preparation that such a change in era deserves.

Figure 1.1: Industrial Revolutions 1 to 4

INDUSTRY 1.0	INDUSTRY 2.0	INDUSTRY 3.0	INDUSTRY 4.0
Steam power Mechanization	Mass production Electrification	Computing Electronics Automation	Internet of Things Cyber/Physical Systems
Mid/late 1700s → Early 1800s	Late 1800s → First half of 1900s	Second half of 1900s	Early 2000s

In *Exponential Organizations*, Yuri Van Geest outlines how multiple enabling technologies such as 3D printing, industrial robotics, and sensory drone technology have exponentially increased their scale impact (reduced in cost or increased in prevalence) by hundreds, if not thousands, of times, within the last decade alone. As quoted by Graeme Wood and many others since:

Change has never happened this fast before, and it will never be this slow again.

Convergent forces such as digitalization, global inter-connectedness, the numerous ways of getting work done, and consumer and societal changes all point to a dramatic shift in how we work and live.

In this book, we unpack the human and organizational realities presented by these changes and explore practical ideas of how we might take some control to thrive in this new phase, rather than struggle to keep up.

What is the Future of Work, and why does it matter?

To adequately prepare for the changing work environment, just as in any other endeavor, it helps to be clear on the definition of the issue you are trying to solve. It is strange that, amidst all the debate, hype, and commentary on the Future of Work, there is as yet no universally agreed definition of the term.

The "Future of Work" is simply a label of convenience to categorize current and anticipated change to work and the workplace.

It's worth noting also that there is no such "thing" as the Future of Work. It is simply a label of convenience used to categorize every current and anticipated change to work and the workplace. The term is mainly associated and underpinned by the exponential rise of technology driven and enabled change. It covers trends in everything from gig working to automation, robotics, AI, and demographic and generational changes. The term also suggests a semi-distant tomorrow land rather than a current reality, which is another challenge in its communication, relevance and application to day-to-day working life in the present.

But one can't help to feel, particularly as we reflect on the changes that have crept up on us over the last 20 years, that there is something fundamental at play. In truth, while the evidence of change, disruption, and digital enablement of work is everywhere across all sectors and industries, the full impact of these changes has not necessarily "landed" for all. Many traditional aspects and assumptions of working life have continued into the 21st century, causing many at the forefront of new ways of working to claim that, as a wider society, we are still imposing 20th century management structures, mindsets, and solutions onto the very different needs and realities of the present day.

The pandemic forced a global shift, bringing technology-based ways of working further into the mainstream, particularly with the adoption of remote-based or blended working. While dramatic and universal in its speed and impact, the pandemic is, however, only one example of the disruption facing us in the world of work.

Factors and forces at play

Before we take a deeper dive into the impact of the Future of Work on individuals, leaders, and organizations in the chapters ahead, let's take a closer look at some of the trends that contribute to our current state of affairs. The converging forces at play are what Professor Klaus Schwab, founder and executive chairman of the World Economic Forum, coined the "Fourth Industrial Revolution." Unlike previous revolutions, this one:

> ... is characterized by a range of new technologies that are fusing the physical, digital, and biological worlds, impacting all disciplines, economies, and industries, and even challenging ideas about what it means to be human.

Schwab suggests this new revolution:

> ... requires nothing less than the transformation of humankind.

Table 1.1 details some of the concrete trends and drivers behind such a dramatic conclusion.

The level and pace of organizational change, technology development, skills shortages and disruption to how and where work gets done presents significant consequences, challenges and opportunities – and ultimately choices – for us as individuals, organizations, and for wider society in general.

Table 1.1: Future of Work Drivers

DRIVERS	KEY FEATURES
Technology and Hyper-connectivity	o Digital and mobile; the "connectivity culture" o Human/Machine augmentation, cyber physical systems
Demographic & Societal Change	o Longevity; the "participation society;" individualism *versus* collectivism; increasing customer sophistication and demands; rapid urbanization
Rapid Business Change	o Globalization; the "knowledge economy;" corporate social responsibility
Changing Work and Workplace	o Changing expectations from workers and employers about what, when, where, and how work gets done o An increasing variety of alternative ways for work to be done, including automation and flexible work methods o Diversity and Inclusion
Energy, Resources & Health	o Climate change, resource scarcity, leading towards renewables and sustainability. o Management of global health care and solutions

Schwab, amongst others, calls for leaders and wider society to:

> *… shape a future that works for all by putting people first, empowering them, and constantly reminding ourselves that all of these new technologies are first and foremost tools made by people for people.*

This sentiment reminds us that, while change is happening at speed, we need to reflect on what it means and to gain *some* control of it. We need to ensure that work and working life is going in a direction that we want and need for future generations to thrive and we need to continue to shape it in a progressive way for everyone. To borrow a phrase used by organizations such as the UN, OECD, and others regarding the next phase for society and work: "Let no one be left behind." This is perhaps a key principle to keep in mind as the so-called Future of Work continues to unfold.

Six realities from inside the Future of Work

Through our work over recent years in helping leaders and organizations unwrap and make sense of the Future of Work for their specific circumstances, six clear and irrefutable realities always emerge that need to be stitched into organizational planning and strategies for the future:

1. We are dealing with greater complexity and ambiguity on an ongoing basis.
2. There is more rapid and continuous business model disruption.
3. We need to deliver on short-term strategies and priorities, while also sensing and scanning for future possibilities.
4. There are increasing options for how and where work gets done.
5. Work and workplace expectations are changing fast.
6. Agility is required as an on-going, sustainable capability, not just an episodic, sporadic or *ad hoc* quality as it has been largely regarded in the past.

To capture these realities into a working definition for the Future of Work, I have found the following to be a useful short-hand version:

... the Future of Work is the fusion of rapid business adaptability, organizational agility, and fundamental changes to work and the workplace.

With a working definition of the Future of Work in hand, and the six irrefutable realities associated with it, it is possible to be more proactive in planning and preparing our organizations and ourselves for the rapidly changing workforce and workplace. Clarity and consensus on the problem we are seeking to solve will help leaders and individuals to understand and evaluate the practical implications of the Future of Work and what it means in reality. More clarity on what we are trying to achieve also will help us understand the roles that need to be played by organizations, leaders, and employees – as well as by policy-makers and society as a whole – to make the new work environment successful for all, and not just the few.

Implications for individuals, leaders and organizations

While the debate and components of the broader impact to organizations will continue, a number of clear factors dominate the commentary regarding the *human* impact of the Future of Work and the changing workplace. These factors directly affect all of us in relation to how, when, and where we will work in the years to come.

The role of technology in our personal and working lives

Technological advances such as cloud computing, deep learning, robotics, and sensory technology are fundamentally changing both the supply side of how, what, where and when work can be done, as well as the demand side in terms of increasing customer expectations and the emergence of globally accessible products and services. While technological advancement undoubtedly impacts existing jobs, other jobs and skills are equally emerging all the time. This period of adjustment will need to be proactively managed so that the new (and existing) jobs are accessible for those most impacted by the Fourth Industrial Revolution. But individuals also need to be aware of the shifting nature of work so they can equip themselves for the inevitable changes ahead.

In *The Second Machine Age*, Erik Brynjolfsson and Andrew McAfee capture this mix of concern and opportunity for current and prospective employees facing the Future of Work:

> *There has never been a better time to be a worker with special skills or the right education, because these people can use technology to create and capture value. However, there's never been a worse time to be a worker with only "ordinary" skills and abilities to offer, because computers, robots, and other digital technologies are acquiring these skills and abilities at an extraordinary rate.*

International connectivity

Globalization is not a new phenomenon but it has been greatly accelerated by greater connectivity and the insatiable appetite of organizations and countries for growth and access to new markets, products and supply chains. While periodic political movements perhaps check this trend in the name of national sovereignty and protectionism, the reality is that technology enabled and customer driven global trade will continue to develop and evolve at pace. International connectedness has led to a genuine global citizenship, which impacts individuals in terms of how, where, and when they work.

Demographic changes & the changing workplace

For a rapidly increasing number of people work can now be done at any time and from anywhere (technology permitting). Knowledge workers can decide who they will work for and how. In many countries, people are living and working longer, leading to multi-generational workplaces, as well as the challenges and costs associated with managing an aging workforce. Societal attitudes and expectations about work and working life are increasingly changing and work is evolving as something you do, not where you go.

New models of work

New work options, supported and abetted by a new generation of workers and enabled by big tech and data, have entered the equation. Robotics, AI, gig working, talent platforms, and volunteerism are now norms for the execution and delivery of work. The changing nature of work demands a different approach to how work is organized and evaluated.

Consequently, as John Kotter, the authority on change, said:

> *Traditional hierarchical structures and organizational processes …*
> *are no longer up to the task of winning in this fast-moving world.*

Even back in 2016, Deloitte reported that organizational design was the number one issue for senior executives and HR leaders worldwide: 92% rated it as a key priority. Disruptive innovation and fast-paced global market accessibility were forcing companies to be adaptable to ensure they could deliver to their increasingly demanding and diverse customer base.

The speed and complexity of change

Terms such as "blitzscaling," "Agile" and "Scrum" from the manufacturing and software sectors are synonymous with rapid and continuous change – but now are entering the lexicon of modern management and human resource management. As American strategic management scholar Rita McGrath points out:

… to win in volatile and uncertain environments, executives need to learn how to exploit short-lived opportunities with speed and decisiveness …

… and to be able to rapidly:

… jump from the maturity stage of one business to the growth stage of the next.

The increased speed and pace of change is accompanied by greater uncertainty as to the eventual outcomes, which requires individuals to react quickly in a work environment that has greater ambiguity to it than ever before. Such implications go to the heart of the realities of the Future of Work. It is clear, therefore, that we need to incorporate these factors into our assumptions about work and our career strategies for the future.

A new era in work and working life

All the evidence from the Future of Work debate suggests the continued fragmentation of traditional employment models. Relatively secure jobs, pensions, and steady employment prospects will give way to a more splintered and varied world of work – heralding the need for a new social and employment contract (further explored later in **Chapter 8**).

The Industrial Revolution brought about a new employment model, which evolved from – and largely replaced – the mainly agricultural, laborer, and artisan self-employment existence. This was followed by a necessary "correction period" when new forms of employee welfare and processes were created to support a more balanced and fair employment model, striking a better balance between the employer and the employee. In the last half of the 20th century, this development was accelerated as employers grappled with attracting and retaining key talent and, simultaneously, sought new models to outsource labor and save costs. Similarly, for our new phase of work, there will be a need for new norms, strategies, and checks and balances to ensure that employees' needs and prospects for the future are as well served as those of their employer.

The pace of change and adoption of new technology does not match the time it typically takes for humans to adapt to change as a whole. Organizational design, therefore, will require a more deliberate and planned focus on the adaptive qualities necessary at both the organizational and individual level – and also for this adaptiveness to happen at a greater and ongoing pace than ever before. History shows that this kind of change is possible and there are many examples of organizations that have taken a proactive role in preparing both their business models and their workforces for such change. Take the case of AT&T in how it set about a multi-year program of transformation in order to prepare itself and its workforce for the new digital world and market place it faced.

Heraclitus, the ancient Greek philosopher, is famous for saying, "Change is the only constant in life." Future changes will come at us with more frequency and speed than in previous cycles, and individual employees will also need to assume greater control of their own career and skills destiny.

Where do we go from here?

In this chapter, we have looked at the forces, realities, and key impacts involved in the Future of Work, most of which are already recorded and well known. However, many commentators believe that, if left unchecked, the "Uberization of work" or the upsurge in the "gig economy" could have potential social and economic downsides; particularly if the efficiency-oriented and cost-reducing business models become the norm in wider society.

Case in Point 1.1: AT&T

Background

AT&T, one of America's largest and most iconic telecom infrastructure companies, faced the reality of a rapidly transforming digital marketplace; a transformation of jobs and skills needs for the future. Rather than a traditional strategy of exiting legacy roles and hiring in-demand talent from the outside, AT&T undertook an ambitious, longer sighted program – "Workforce 2020" – to upskill and reskill its 250,000 people.

Key Take-aways

o An organization-wide skill gap audit allowed the company to identify how it could develop and source required skills internally rather than relying on external sources.

o HR processes, such as development and performance management, were revamped to promote development of in-demand skills.

o An online self-service platform that included a career profile to identify an employee's skill gap, a career intelligence tool to provide employees better stats on hiring trends within the organization, and a job simulation tool that allowed employees to deal with practice situations in new jobs were accessed more than six million times in a period of a year.

o AT&T encouraged upskilling / reskilling through a variety of courses and qualifications in partnership with Georgia Tech and Udacity.

o The company shifted from the traditional upward career path to a lattice career path that allows employees to keep skills relevant, improves opportunities for development, and increases inclusivity throughout the organization.

o The upskilling and change program was done through an open and honest dialogue with employees and representatives regarding future skills needs and the changing nature of jobs and the industry at large.

Sources

AT&T's radical Talent Overhaul: https://hbr.org/2016/10/atts-talent-overhaul.
The Keys to AT&T's SAFE Transformation: https://soundcloud.com/agileamped/the-keys-to-atts-safe-transformation.

Martin Ford, for example, warns of soaring inequality, increasing unemployment, and underemployment if the full potential of technological advancement proceeds unabated without mindful policy and structural change.

On the positive side, such advances in technology and organizational flexibility have brought and will continue to bring significant benefits in all fields of human life, such as easier access to education and advances in healthcare. The technologically enabled "democratization of work" heralds new possibilities for how and where people can work and participate in a fast-changing economy.

But what does the inside of the Future of Work look like for those who are already there? And, given the importance of work to society as a whole, what does it mean for us as well as for educators, policy-makers and government as a whole? We will examine these questions in greater detail in the pages ahead.

What You Can Do
On the individual level:

- How does the definition of the Future of Work and the key factors underpinning it affect you?
- What is your plan for Future of Work readiness?

On the organizational level:

- How does the definition of the Future of Work as presented in this chapter impact and affect your organization?
- Compare your organization against the six Future of Work realities and identify practical actions you can take to improve these underlying capabilities for your team and the wider organization.

Chapter 2
THE CASE FOR AGILITY

It is not the most intellectual of the species that survives; it is not the strongest that survives; but the species that survives is the one that is able to adapt to and to adjust best to the changing environment in which it finds itself.

Charles Darwin

As we all know from Darwin's well-worn quote, agility is nothing new. And when it comes to individuals, leaders and organizations successfully adapting to the ever-changing Future of Work, leading researchers such as Ashutosh Muduli are also in no doubt as to the underlying competency we all need to have:

Agility is the most predominant solution to the problem of adapting to unpredictable, dynamic, and constantly changing business environments.

In *Mastering Turbulence*, authors Joseph McCann and John Selsky also identify agility at the organizational, team, and individual level as the most common and necessary quality to deal with "rapid and turbulent change." And, in her book *The Agile Organization*, Linda Holbeche notes:

Business leaders and individuals will need to adopt Agile
practices and mindsets in order to thrive in this new landscape.

The good news is that it is within everyone's power to become
more agile. As it turns out, we humans have been doing it for
many years! As a species we have continued to learn how to think
more flexibly; to sense, shift and adapt to new circumstances as
they inevitably arise. Agility is what has already enabled us to
successfully adapt over the millennia. But agility now has a new
context in the Future of Work – and it needs a fresh look to help
us adapt to the increasing pace and complexity of working life.
Agility needs to be a more enduring, deliberate, and conscious
mindset and skillset, not just an episodic, adaptive and reactive
measure that we rely on in times of material risk or opportunity.

Why agility?

The important relationship between agility and the Future of Work
readiness was confirmed through extensive research conducted by
our leadership and organization consultancy group, WorkMatters.
This award-winning research explored the origins and practical
implications of organizational agility and specifically looked at the
individual qualities and skills most associated with successfully
adapting to rapidly changing work environments.

Organizations are now adopting agility as a *deliberate* strategy rather than as an episodic necessity.

Our original primary research took place over a two-year period and involved extensive interviews with business owners and HR leaders representing over 150,000 employees from a range of small, large, local and multinational organizations. The findings of this research have since been tested, validated, and applied within organizations and with professionals in the agility field from all around the world.

Over 90% of the leaders in our field research "strongly agreed" that agility was a critical component in being Future of Work ready. The others "agreed" with the statement but pointed out that it may not be critical for *every* individual to be agile, depending on their role and the activities they perform in the organization. For those employees, however, all leaders agreed that *not having an agile mindset* could expose them to the risks of automation or the effects of redundancy in the future landscape of work.

In his published research, Ashutosh Muduli also outlined how organizations are adopting agility as a *deliberate* strategy to thrive and survive in an increasingly complex and changing business environment rather than just as a desired state called on in times of emergency and opportunity. His research, and that of others, confirms the centrality of organizational agility in the Future of Work debate. The argument is simple and compelling: if business leaders can build agility into the organizational culture, structure, and processes, they will have made significant strides in preparing their organization for the challenges and opportunities ahead.

Though the case for agility may be clear, that doesn't necessarily make it easy to practice or implement on the organizational or personal level. There is no magic "agility switch" we can turn on simply because we want to. But throughout this book we will look at agility from a number of different perspectives to help you progress the topic from a desired or aspired outcome to actual reality and daily practice.

Fundamentally, agility is necessary to confront *complexity*, which is at the core of the challenges we face in the Future of Work and modern working life in general. Based on the work of complexity theory and agility experts such as Ralph Stacey, Brenda Zimmerman, Dave Snowden, and others, **Figure 2.1** is useful to understand the moving parts we are dealing with when it comes to complexity and how agility can help us.

This theory suggests that, as the pace of change and uncertainty increases, we need to find ways to deal with increasing complexity. In previous economic cycles, where these forces were not as prevalent, we could more readily "plan and control" our organizational strategies or individual careers. Different skillsets and mindsets are required to operate in the two different environments, hence the agility challenge. We need to be able to operate in both the stable, plan and control world and in the more adaptive, complex world – often at the same time – with the possibility of the occasional visit into "chaos" as well!

**Figure 2.1: Increased Pace of Change +
Uncertainty = Complexity**

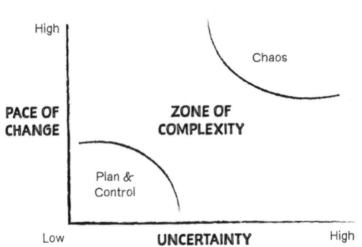

Management consultants McKinsey and Mercer have referred to agility as the ambidextrous quality of being both stable and flexible when the environment and situation requires. This quality allows for the ability to focus and execute effectively in the present, while being able to sense, respond, and adapt to changes and conditions on the horizon. As one CEO from the insurance industry pointed out in our research:

> *In the fast moving but also regulated and transparent world we are in, we are looking at a greater need than ever before for standardization/control one day and the ability to turn on a pin the next ...*

As humans, we do this quite intuitively anyway, yet the CEO's observation sums up the paradox of the new working world. This is why agility has become one of the most common terms in the lexicon of business thinking and strategy design over the past decade or two. In more recent times, the COVID-19 pandemic experience provided everyone with a very real example and reference point for what agility looks like on an organizational and individual level when it is called upon literally overnight.

To help organizations and individuals effectively prepare for the Future of Work, it is therefore worthwhile to understand (and more deliberately apply) the core competency of agility a bit further.

Organizational agility defined

Historically, and as can be seen playing out today, the first issue with agility is its definition, just as it is with the Future of Work. In order to change or move towards something, we need to be clear on what it is we are seeking to change or move towards.

One HR leader in our research put it this way:

> *If we can first de-code together what agility really means in practice, for us and our context, we then have some chance in making it happen through our structures, processes, and people practices.*

The *Cambridge Dictionary* defines agility as:

> *... being able to move quickly and easily ... being able to think quickly and clearly.*

Academics Chyan Yang and Hsian-Ming Liu summarized the current academic thinking:

> *Enterprise agility is a complex, multi-dimensional, and context specific concept, comprised of the ability to sense environmental change and quickly respond to unprecedented change by flexibly assembling resources, processes, knowledge, and capabilities.*

With so many contributing factors embodied in the single concept of agility, no wonder it tends to be inconsistently defined and understood. There is a lot going on in a very small word. I find a simple and useful analogy for agility to be like that of a snow skier – skillfully focusing, negotiating, and responding to immediate and current obstacles in the present, while simultaneously scanning for opportunity and risk further ahead – and all at speed.

A skier's skill goes beyond flexibility. A steady core of stability is also required: strength, skill, and competence. Like skiing, agility implies a forward-looking, positive orientation, adjusting course towards an ultimate goal, responding to threat and opportunity along the way.

Despite the challenges of universally defining and researching such a multi-layered concept, significant effort has been made to implement summarized models and commonly-held interpretations of agility enhancing capabilities. These include agility enabling activities such as scenario modeling, generating operational flexibility, and developing agile practices.

Table 2.1 summarizes the most common characteristics of organizational agility encountered in our research over several years with business and HR leaders, as well as within the literature.

Business leaders commonly confirmed change orientation, speed, and learning orientation as key elements of organizational agility. They noted the importance of structure and process. Furthermore, the themes of culture and mindset that emerged from our research confirmed that the concept of sustainable organizational agility is a deeply-rooted and culture-enabled approach, as opposed to just a tactical initiative, methodology, or clearly mapped out process. This reflects why those in the Agile movement (see next section) often distinguish between *doing* Agile *versus* really *being* Agile.

In order to capture the essence of Agility at enterprise level, and to illustrate the contrast to a more "traditional" organizational approach, consultants, and practitioners use diagrams such as **Figure 2.2** to convey some of the themes involved.

Table 2.1: Common Factors in Defining Organizational Agility

FACTORS	ELEMENTS & QUALITIES
Flexibility and responsiveness	o Sensing and openness to external environment o Inquisitive o Responsive internal response
Adaptability and change orientation	o Internal responsivity and change capacity o Well-tuned change capability and orientation o Efficient coping with changing conditions o Comfortable with ambiguity
Fast	o Focus on action and rate/speed, relative to competition and traditional norms
Intentional	o Signal of deliberate response and not *ad hoc* reaction to once-off crisis or opportunity o Anticipatory and open *versus* purely reactive
Dynamic	o Dexterous, nimble, energetic and focused, more than internal or external norm
Innovative use of resources, including others	o Creative use of resources/knowledge o Open to creating something new and to collaboration with other parties
Learning orientation	o Learning evident, open to risk, sharing and transfer of knowledge for further use

Figure 2.2: Traditional *versus* Agile Organizations

	TRADITIONAL Organization	AGILE Organization
Strategy	Top-down vision, purpose and strategy	Shared vision, purpose and strategy
Design	Designed primarily for stability	Designed for stability and dynamism
Structure	Hierarchical and siloed	Networked, flat and cross-functional
Planning	Linear and sequential	Iterative and dynamic
Culture	Hierarchical, top-down, controlling, goals and delegations cascade	Collaborative, local accountability and execution Open mindset, iterative, rapid experimentation and learning

The roots of Agile

Without straying too deeply into historical territory best left to others, the concept of organizational agility is historically associated with developments in continuous improvement such as Lean manufacturing. With roots as a deliberate strategy that can be arguably traced back to the 1930s, and often used interchangeably with the concept of flexibility, agility was generally defined as "the ability to manage supply and demand uncertainties." As noted in the work by Dr. John McMackin and others, the agile concept today operates at multiple levels and across multiple sectors– from philosophy, culture and mindset, through to processes and methodologies.

It was particularly popularized in the 1990s in the software industry, the "Agile movement" appeared as a way to improve productivity and customer centricity in what was a rapidly changing technology environment. By 2001, traditional linear or "waterfall" methods in the software development arena originating over previous decades had simply become unsustainable due to increasing business demands and expectations. The explosion in technological advancement, specifically from the Internet, underpinned that unsustainability.

Sustainable organizational agility is a deeply-rooted and culture-enabled approach.

At a gathering in Snowbird, Utah, 17 software developers came together and crafted a document known as the *Agile Manifesto*. The *Manifesto* was arguably a line in the sand. While various Agile practices had been developing for some years, the *Manifesto* acknowledged that "something had to change" in how work could be delivered. It was a clear statement of intent to recalibrate two moving parts – the pace of change, customer demands and adaptability on one hand, and a new working style and set of principles on the other. These guideposts began to take hold in accommodating the new reality of dealing with increased complexity and rapidly changing and evolving circumstances particularly within the software and product development fields where those conditions often prevailed. More recently, this is now relevant and connected to wider enterprise change, particularly with the onset of digital transformation and other business disruptions.

The evolution of the technology and software sectors is an important story for all of us who care about the practical realities of the Future of Work. It makes sense that, in a technology driven revolution such as the age we are now in, that these sectors would be the first to experience the sharp end and implications of the disruption to their work and work practices. The context and conditions first faced by the technology community now also resonate with wider organizational realities and working life today. Their experience of and need for agility has now extended into the broader business context. Their practices have also been recognized as a useful set of capabilities for rapid response to market changes and to cope with unexpected change in a flexible but disciplined manner.

Agility versus *Agile*

A nuance worth considering however is the "agility *versus* agile" question, which we frequently encounter in our work. 'Agile' has presented the broader theme of agility with somewhat of a PR or image challenge. Sometimes, the basic argument and case for agility gets too caught up in a debate as to whether or not you subscribe to the principles, practices, and methods of the popular "Agile" movement.

The "Agile" approach, tools, and methods have evolved – and continue to evolve – as a valuable set of multi-disciplinary, customer centered and collaborative practices designed to help enable agility within teams and organizations, but the two ideas are not necessarily joined at the hip. We have observed plenty of agile organizations that do not employ what might be considered standard "Agile" methods and practices. While the underlying principles may be common, their ways of working are built from their own adaptive tools and practices over time. And there are plenty of organizations that employ "Agile" methods that still struggle with creating genuine agility across the enterprise.

Agility and agile are two separate but clearly related concepts. The higher purpose and goal of creating agility in our organizational and professional lives is paramount for today's rapidly changing environment and for Future of Work readiness – whether or not you subscribe to the "Agile" toolkit and practices. Agile can definitely help with the journey but agility is the ultimate prize and a case like Hilcorp Energy outlined at the end of this chapter is perhaps an example.

The continued evolution of disciplines such as Agile also reflect an increased crossover of historically separate but logically interdependent concepts such as lean process development and wider management theory and organizational culture.

Researcher and author Dr. John McMackin has observed in his work how the disciplines such as lean and agile and wider management theory have slowly begun (at last) to converge. He notes that:

Responsibility for implementation of lean in many ways reflects its origins in the engineering divisions of industry, particularly car manufacturers, so that lean initiatives in manufacturing settings still tend to be led by engineers, or their equivalent in service businesses. This shows up in a tendency to over-emphasize the technical aspects of lean implementation to the neglect of the social and human aspects including culture, leadership and the psychology of change. Many researchers believe this explains the relatively high levels of reported failure of such initiatives to deliver fully on expected and sustainable results.

The agility challenge

The challenges and issues of implementing agility therefore can be categorized into three main points:

- The relatively ill-defined and inconsistent nature of organizational agility;
- Its complexity when it comes to practical execution and implementation;
- Lack of focused attention to how it is being applied in practice from both the academic and the business worlds.

Although we defined organizational agility in a previous section, business leaders in our research struggled to provide a single or succinct definition of the term; reminiscent of how we have often struggled to capture a common understanding of other phenomena such as culture and employee engagement. This is more than a matter of semantics. It is an issue for operationalizing the concept further; for communicating and applying it successfully in a consistent and meaningful way for all involved in their specific context. If business leaders do not agree on a formal and consistent definition of agility that works for them, it will be challenging to conceive, communicate, and implement policy and practices across the organization in a cohesive way.

The ill-defined nature of organizational agility poses a challenge to the rigor and consistency of the underlying research and its applicability from one context to another. The concern is that, without further work on a robust definition and theoretical construct for agility, it will remain an elusive or faddish concept.

Secondly, the issues arising from the complexity of the construct and application of agility include:

- The conflicting trade-offs required between speed and magnitude of response;
- Balancing the sometimes contradictory or paradoxical nature of sustainable operational and environmental practices with the immediacy of short-term business demands; and
- Limiting factors associated with agility, such as organizational age and size.

The context-sensitive nature of agility is stressed frequently in research literature, while the complex interdependency of the agility concepts (culture, workforce, organizational abilities and technology) is also widely noted.

The final challenge is that organizational agility has not received sufficient, coherent and focused attention in either academia or the practical world – although this is rapidly changing. For example, an Economist Intelligence Unit survey of CEOs and CIOs found that 90% agreed on the importance of agility for future business success and survival.

Furthermore, a McKinsey Global Survey identified that:

- Organizational agility was a top priority or within top-three priorities for three-quarters of the respondents;
- 81% of respondents in agile units reported a significant or moderate increase in performance since their transformation began;
- Agile units are 1.5 times more likely to outperform their peers in financial performance.

MIT's CIO research noted that agile firms grow revenue 37% faster and generate 30% higher profits than non-agile companies. In its *2020 Global Report*, the Business Agility Institute demonstrated how more agile organizations had adapted more quickly and more effectively to the pandemic than other firms – simply because they had already developed the agility "muscle" and mindset. As noted by Evan Leybourn, the co-founder and CEO of the Business Agility Institute:

> *Throughout the COVID-19 pandemic, our research showed that a primary distinguishing factor of organizations that were able to respond to the disruptive events and thrive was that these were organizations for whom agility had already been developed as a core capability.*

While the business case for agility may be clear, there often exists a natural conflict or tension between agile practical practices and principles (whatever they may be for you) and the more traditional, familiar, and often successful ways of working of the past. In terms of leadership attention, more pressing, short-term challenges can remain higher up on the priority list. However, given the compelling adaptive and future-proofing benefits that come with agility, its prominence on the strategic, organizational and talent agenda is likely to increase as traditional organizational work models become even more disrupted and unsustainable into the future.

While perhaps uncomfortable at first, particularly for those of us from traditional command and control origins, it seems we will just have to embrace the tricky paradoxes and messy contradictions that agility brings. It also seems clear that agility needs to exist and be addressed throughout the different levels and layers of the organization, and not just simply as a concept that is understood and applied in one department, team, or function (see **Figure 2.3**). We will explore agility through these various lenses throughout the book.

Figure 2.3: The Levels and Components of Organizational Agility

ORGANISATIONAL AGILITY
- Strategy and Culture
- Structure and Processes
- Technology
- Workforce and HR Practices
- Learning and Customer Mindset

TEAM AGILITY
- Shared Goals and Alignment
- Agile Processes, Problem Solving, and Decision Making
- Supportive Relationships
- Accountability

PERSONAL AGILITY
- Personal // Individual

The prime source of agility

To achieve Future of Work readiness and agility at the leadership or organizational level, I believe we must start at the personal, individual level to help us make sense of it. Ultimately, this is the source of any agile team or organization. What is an organization anyway but a collection of individuals?

In previous generations of working life, we might have simply directed people to operate in a certain way – but not today. For sustainable performance and outcomes, individuals need to be convinced and invested in the benefits of behaving differently. They also need to have a supportive environment where behavioral change is safe, encouraged, and recognized.

If we can understand the human dimension of agility, if we can develop the ability at the individual level to "be agile" rather than to just "do agile," and then we can address the challenges and solutions required at team and organizational levels. It will also help us as individuals to thrive in this fast-moving and pressurized environment by future-proofing our careers. If we don't address the human factor, then we won't obtain the personal benefits of agility. And our efforts at the organizational level – in terms of implementing agile processes, practices, and structures – ultimately will be, on their own, in vain.

Look at any organizational priority and the issue is the same. We all want to have "engaged" employees and a positive organizational "culture." But we have learned from years of hard earned experience that these aspired states rarely come from top--down initiatives, strategies, and processes alone. The must-win battle is at individual level, where enough people in the organization voluntarily and individually genuinely see the benefits and buy into the target concept and state themselves.

John Kotter, author of *Organizational Change*, discovered in his vast work in this area that, while we talk about influencing hearts and minds in change initiatives, the vast majority of time and effort is spent on the mind part (logic), not the heart part (emotional buy-in). This omission results in only the partial success, or even the ultimate failure, of the change being sought. Authentic buy-in comes through individual interactions, behaviors, and attitudes. People make micro individual decisions, on a day-to-day basis, that ultimately convert into the desired organizational outcomes such as engagement, positive cultural expression, and, in this case, agility.

Where do we go from here?

In this chapter we have explored the critical but tricky subject of agility, a necessary Future of Work strategy and a capability that demands both flexibility and control. It requires the dual ability to focus on short-term delivery, while also sensing and responding to changing circumstances. The agility imperative is too important to overlook, and ignoring it because we don't like the term or because it seems hard or unpleasant won't make it go away. Call it something else if you like – adaptability, flexibility, deftness – as many do, but ultimately the constituent elements and practical skills associated with agility need to be understood and applied if we are all to thrive in the Future of Work.

In the pages that follow, we will explore and illustrate the agility topic in a way that will hopefully help individuals, leaders, and organizations move agility from a vague, hopeful aspiration to a lived and operational reality. As we discovered in our research and in observing the habits of successful agile leaders and individuals, *mindset* is ultimately a critical starting point to adopting agility and ensuring Future of Work readiness on a personal, leadership, and organizational level. We will explore personal agility, through the lens of individual mindset and the skillset that accompanies it, in the next two chapters.

Case in Point 2.1: Hilcorp Energy

Background

Hilcorp Energy, a private oil and gas company, specializes in taking over complicated, legacy assets and maximizing their output. The company consistently ranks the highest in Great Place to Work surveys. Hilcorp is an example of an organization working with an agile mindset and approach without reference to any specific agile methodology or practices – it is just naturally bred in its culture and way of doing business.

Key Take-aways

o Driven by a clear set of values and a number of key practices – flat organization, delegation and alignment of goals and incentives – Hilcorp has created a culture of ownership and accountability amongst employees for the success of the team and the business. The goal is to foster an entrepreneurial organization with clear accountabilities, a focus on value, and the ability to act quickly.
o The company is divided into multi-disciplinary, cross-functional asset teams that work directly with the legacy assets. They organize themselves autonomously and are accountable for the success of the project. The rest of the organization works together to support the work of these teams.
o Work is delegated down to the people who have the most direct contact with the asset (rather than management), in this case the foremen and field employees. Maximum number of levels above any employee is five.
o Targets are closely aligned; incentives are given to every employee if the organization as a whole meets these targets. Annual bonuses are the same for every person in the organization.
o Mandatory processes are minimal and exist to increase productivity, not restrict it. Core values also guide the organization's processes.

Sources

https://www.mckinsey.com/business-functions/organization/our-insights/digging-deep-for-organizational-innovation
https://www.hilcorp.com/about-us/corporate-culture/

What you can do

On the individual level:

- What is your own personal working definition of agility?
- How could a clearer understanding of agility benefit you and your future career?
- What challenges might it present to you and how might you overcome them?

On the organizational level:

- What is your team's working definition of agility? How can you best relate the concept to your team and your organization?
- How agile is your organization? What evidence or examples do you have for both agile and non-agile aspects of your organization?
- What are the main gaps between where you are with that definition and where you would like to be?
- What actions might help to close such gaps at organizational, team, leadership and individual level?

Part Two

PERSONAL AGILITY

Chapter 3
THE AGILE MINDSET

Between stimulus and response there is a space.
In that space is our power to choose our response.
In our response lies our growth and our freedom.
Viktor E. Frankl

When you break agility down to its most fundamental elements, it is really about change and our relationship with change. At the individual level, we all know agility when we see it. Some people just seem to be able to easily and positively adapt and adjust to changing circumstances. They're happy to experiment with new ways of doing things, and they're open to learning, change and collaboration. For them, the glass always seems half full rather than half empty. Others are more fixed in their ways and struggle with change. They're happier approaching work as they have in the past, generally relying on the habits, patterns and knowledge that has served them well, but they then find it difficult when disruption hits.

Why is it that adapting to change is easy for some people and significantly harder for others? A big part of the answer lies with our mindset. And, for those who struggle with change (and therefore agility), what is needed to shift their mindset so that change feels more comfortable, positive and normal.

Global experts and best-selling authors on the subject such as Stephen Denning, Carol Dweck, Ahmed Sidky, Pia-Mia Thorén, Natal Dank and others, have all pointed in different ways to the primacy of mindset as a foundational ingredient for personal agility. According to these experts, a certain mental inclination, positively disposed towards behaving with agility or being agile, and a conviction as to why it is of benefit to act in an agile way, are fundamental prerequisites for us to be able to adopt agile principles and practices and ultimately to thrive in complex, frequently changing work environments. As one CEO told me as part of our research for this book:

Agility comes from mindset. I can train for skills and processes, but if the mental attitude is not there, it is not going to happen.

This is no different than other examples of human behavior and performance I have encountered in my experience of coaching, leadership development, and talent management over the years. How often do we hear of someone achieving this or failing at that due to their mindset? When the mindset is strong and focused and committed, it seems like nothing is impossible.

While the emphasis on mindset is intuitively compelling, too often it is another idea thrown about as a convenient, catch-all explanation without much consideration of what it actually means – or how it can be developed. How can our mindset help us succeed in any goal or state we care to pursue, agility and Future of Work readiness being cases in point?

In this chapter, we will look at what mindset is and why it matters. In the next chapter, we will look at the more visible skills associated with personal agility. We argue that mindset and skillset are essentially two sides of the same coin and surely an important combination to better understand.

The dance of personal change

As noted above, when we consider the practical, human implications of agility, it ultimately comes down our relationship with change. Personally, I don't care much for change. If I'm honest, I don't really like it at all. Learning a new skill or process, starting a job, changing a long-term habit that I know is not serving me well – it all feels quite hard at first. My initial reaction to a "new" idea is like the inevitable groan from my teenage son when asked to do a chore on a Saturday afternoon.

Our deep-rooted feelings about change are evidence of our mindset at play. Indeed, our nervous system's initial response is to defend itself from "attack" – so our instinct is to preserve energy and keep things the way they are. For some, being able to break through this initial resistance towards achieving their goal is just what they do and who they are. Like the entrepreneur who doesn't get put off by early setbacks or lack of knowledge or lack of resources in trying and pursuing something new, they seem to have an optimism and belief in what they are about. They believe that things will turn out and will be OK. Others see the same opportunity, but the hurdle, effort and price of discomfort and change involved in grasping that opportunity is greater than the comfortable benefits of keeping things the way they are. It's one of those paradoxes where the same, life-saving quality and instinct of self-preservation and protection from harm also can be what holds us back from growth and positive change.

Thriving in the Future of Work, however, demands that we be more conscious, skillful, and deliberate about how we change – and why. We need to know more about our own mindset so that we can read our own reactions and "change signals" in a given situation. This self-awareness will help us to adapt with greater purpose, ease and control rather than just drift and react as if we are on some kind of mental autopilot.

The science bit

Changing habits and behaviors has been the subject of extensive research for over 100 years. Early studies on how the nervous system and brain functions in the fields of behavioral theory, emotional intelligence, neuroplasticity, and cybernetics have explored how we can more deliberately and consciously control our thoughts and behaviors to bring about a desired outcome.

Cathy O'Grady, an executive coach and consultant, who works with her clients on personal change, describes how this deeper understanding of the science of change can help:

> So often people I am working with say they want to change but struggle with making the necessary changes happen. Knowing the natural process of change encourages them to be more deliberate, determined and planned in their own change journey and to achieve the benefits they seek.

With so much external stimulation, demand for our attention and continuous change, experts in the field, such as Dr. Andrew Huberman, Neuroscientist and Professor of Neurobiology at Stanford University, help us understand the brain's natural process in making sense of and navigating the environment we are in. Huberman is also a colleague of Carol Dweck, who successfully popularized the relevant idea of having a "growth mindset" as opposed to a "fixed mindset" as a key enabler of learning and growth. Huberman (and others) study how the chemicals and circuitry in our brains deal with change and our reaction to our experiences and our environment. He explores how, when considering change big or small, we can steady ourselves, deal with the initial and necessary discomfort and agitation involved, and then successfully set out on our path towards the change we seek, whether that is going for a jog, developing a new skill, writing a book, or running for office – the same circuitry responses are deployed each time. I'm sure

Huberman and his colleagues would rightly say there is more complexity involved, but the following three steps cover the basic neurochemistry involved.

Step 1: Focus: Alertness, focus, and urgency

The process of internal change begins when we bring conscious thinking and focus to the change we either encounter, need or desire. When confronted by a change, or any stimulus, a stress-oriented alertness response is triggered (through the adrenaline norepinephrine). This is a protective and defensive response, and it's the cause of initial suspicion, agitation, or resistance to the "threat" of the new idea or stimulus. This is normal; the brain is being mobilized for action. It is the same chemical reaction that protects us from danger and makes us the successful species we are.

The organic chemical, acetylcholine, from deep inside the brain (*nucleus basalis*) then helps us to focus properly on the subject. In doing so, the brain is assessing the requirements and implications of its new challenge in terms of the duration, path, and outcome (DPO): What is this change really about? What does it involve? What are the implications?

The combined work and interaction of alertness and focus is the first and necessary step of any conscious response. The brain places deliberate attention onto something new when it would prefer to default to its more reflexive, relaxed state, hence causing initial discomfort. Again, this is normal and necessary for deliberate action to occur.

While this circuitry (alertness and focus) marks our neural system for change, some form of urgency must accompany it in order to actually push us forward, overcome the natural temptation to reject the new idea, and succumb to the initial agitation and stress. Like getting out of bed in the morning, the combination of alertness, focus, and urgency (or commitment to what we need or seek) is necessary to overcome the resistance to moving forward towards a different state.

Awareness of how to steady our own mental ship and assume control of our thoughts and behaviors is one of the most critical skills we need to develop.

At this point, like a missile fixing on its target, we can move forward. So long as the urgency and desire for the change is there, we progress from good intent to really committing, engaging, or leaning into the change we seek. The adrenaline (acetylcholine) triggers our neuroplasticity and ensures we stay focused on what we seek. The neural pathways strengthen and impress on our subconscious brain that this change is something we want or need to engage with, fueling our resilience and strength against the initial resistance.

Step 2: Act: Action and behavior

This is such an important step. It's like pulling the trigger on the target, or actually going through the motion of getting out of bed! It's when our initial intentions, focus, and newly formed pathways must be quickly transformed into movement and action. The defensive norepinephrine, not happy that it has been alerted to a new path, will tempt us to give up and revert to our more comfortable, previous familiar state but the adrenaline (acetylcholine) helps us keep our focus on the target. Norepinephrine is letting us know that it is still around and ready in case we are under genuine attack. So we are just letting it go to move forward and that it is safe to proceed. In doing so, we are literally changing our physical mindset by giving permission for defensive processes to retreat and for new neural pathways and chemical processes to help us advance. We are, temporarily, consciously incompetent in our early efforts, but our desire and/or urgency to persist towards what we seek or need keeps us going through this early, uncomfortable stage of change.

Then, either through small indications of success and/or the satisfaction that we are on the right road, our body's natural source of reward (dopamine) is triggered. Dopamine gives us the internal energy and encouragement to continue forward, dampening down the resistive power of the defensive/ protective norepinephrine in the process. It is our internal reward system, with our early progress and successes, reassuring us we are on the right path. Indeed, the neural pathways that supported our previous unwanted behavior are weakened and suppressed.

These early steps remind me of a starter's instructions before a race: "On your marks (alertness), get set (focus), go (action)!" The same pattern of alertness, focus, and action is at play in our minds as we get out of the starting blocks towards the change in behavior we want or need to make. And as any runner will tell you, there are always those natural early feelings of agitation and discomfort at the start.

Step 3: Repeat and learn: Alignment, reinforcement, and iteration

With repeated mental commitment and direct action towards the new state we seek, and validation through the results we begin to see, the new neural pathways established earlier in our brains are strengthened even further. We find ourselves operating with a different mindset. Our new actions and habits that serve our goal replace those that don't. Our mindset, confident it is on the right path, seeks continued reward and reinforcement, learning and gathering data from the experience, as it iterates and fine-tunes the new path. Our conscious, sub-conscious, and physical selves are now aligned and operating in a state of conscious competence. This is why many say it takes 21 to 66 days to create a habit (the debate continues). Change will not happen overnight – and it will not happen at all without the pattern of alertness, focus, commitment, behavior modification, reward, reinforcement, and ultimately, competence.

Soon, we don't just see positive change in ourselves alone. Our environment, circumstances, and the response of others also change because we are behaving and engaging differently. This ancient chain reaction between our environment and ourselves was the inspiration behind the insightful quote from 18th century German writer, Johann Wolfgang von Goethe:

At the moment of commitment, the entire universe conspires to assist you.

The *Focus, Act, Repeat,* and *Learn* pattern is essentially a form of neurochemical summary of the age old "dance" of what we know about personal change; the dance between mind and body, aided by our biochemical and nervous systems and our neuroplasticity, in particular. While a child goes through these experiences automatically, due to their natural absorption of what is going on in their environment, adults have to be more deliberate and aware of the process. As adults, we have to understand how to manage the human "wiring" that has developed and settled over the years.

As Huberman says, our minds want to keep playing the same program and mental algorithms, habits, and beliefs that we developed in early life – unless we mindfully and deliberately reprogram our mindsets to do otherwise. To help us do that, knowledge of the body and mind's natural processes outlined above serves to push us through the barriers in our way. Unlocking our mindset and recognizing the brain's micro-steps of change is arguably the key to learning and accepting how to adapt and thrive in the ever-changing Future of Work.

A little experiment

To playfully demonstrate the mental process that goes on in our subconscious, write your first name on a piece of paper as you normally do. How does that simple action feel: comfortable, normal, safe? Change hands and do it again. What thoughts and chatter go through your mind: discomfort, agitation, vulnerability, the desire to stop this nonsense and return to your preferred habit? The latter is simply the early awkward stages of the change process in action. Apply the *Focus, Act, Repeat, and Learn* steps from the previous sections above and notice that after you've committed to *digging in* to the task, the original discomfort and vulnerability subsides. Recognize and acknowledge the thoughts going on, embrace the agitation knowing that it will soon pass, bending to your will to progress towards your goal. You then eventually become more comfortable with what originally felt uncomfortable, awkward or even impossible.

Being aware of the natural process of change is a powerful and empowering step because we know to expect it as a normal, human reaction to that change or disruption. Like any thought, we have a choice as to what we do with it. If negative, we can recognize it for what it is and let it go, rejecting its intention to put us off our course. If positive, we use it to strengthen and reinforce our resolve to move forward. With this awareness, we also know that through repeated action and commitment towards a goal of, say, learning to sign our names with our less dominant hand, or learning a new musical instrument, we can push through the initial agitation and prevail. After gradual progress and with a genuine desire to succeed, the new habit is achieved. And through understanding the science, we can perhaps be more kind to ourselves and others as we initially fall short and struggle with our early efforts. We can then relish the little victories along the way, and stay the course in the pursuit of the ultimate outcomes we want to see.

Mindset: The key to agility and adapting to change

So how does our detour through the neurochemical dance of change in our minds relate to agility? In an environment where change is fast-moving and continuous, and our attention is under constant attack, awareness of how we deal with change and how we can steady our own mental ship and assume control of our thoughts and behaviors is one of the most critical skills we need to develop for the Future of Work. The call to arms for the times we are in is to take notice of how our mindset functions, and to control our reactions to our thoughts about what is going on around us. This will give us the little space we need to process, accept and embrace the struggle between our natural default habits and the proactive formation and creation of new ones that better serve our goals and how we want to be.

Leaders and employees frequently say that agility is hard to grasp as a deliberate skill or approach. It can go against our fixed mindsets and the more familiar, predictable, or linear, patterns of behavior that have served us well in the past. Like any change, or building any new muscle, working with agility can feel awkward, uncertain, and unknown. But the evidence tells us that agility is not just desirable; it is necessary. Also, we have all used our agility muscles before, perhaps just not with the same conscious, deliberate skill and purposeful regularity that we will need to use them in the future.

Knowing a bit more about our relationship with change helps with understanding the challenges that might be involved for people to embrace an agile mindset. For some, this shift will not be as comfortable, instinctive, and natural as it is for others. With change comes a sense of vulnerability and exposure. When it comes to being more agile, we will all have a different response and change journey depending on what is involved for us individually.

I've had the privilege of helping others in one way or another with the agility challenge from a number of professional perspectives over the course of my career. From a business leadership perspective, I've tried to balance those short-term and longer-term priorities, keeping the organization focused on delivery, while also trying to allow room to experiment, fail, prepare, and adjust for the future. I've worked with HR leaders attempting to balance myriad current people issues and programs to ensure corporate consistency, fairness, and compliance, while also trying to build in future flexibility, emerging trends, and individualization. From my leadership development and executive coaching experience, I've seen the individual challenges with agility first-hand from managers and executives. They talk about the increasing pressure to perform and be in the present, while (somehow) sensing future risk and opportunity, which seem to come with increased frequency and impact over time. All of this, while also trying to live a happy and balanced life!

One thing that is abundantly clear from those who effectively and consciously "navigate paradox," as management expert and author David Ulrich eloquently puts it, is that our mindset ultimately makes the difference. It is both as simple and as complex as that.

In his public videos, leadership guru Robin Sharma introduced us to a janitor at Johannesburg airport and was struck by the pride he took in his work without any expectation of extra pay or tips. Struck by this man's attitude, he stopped and talked with him. In their exchange, the janitor spoke about his desire to ensure his "office" was as perfect as it could be. He explained that he saw himself as an important part of his country's welcome to the world; his office was often the first place that most people saw when they touched down in his beloved South Africa. As Sharma says, *"His enthusiasm is utterly contagious. And his impact totally unforgettable."* This is just one of many examples of the empowering and transformative nature of the human mindset. With the right mindset, you can literally bloom wherever you are planted.

This agile mindset is required to help us thrive rather than just cope in the Future of Work.

And so when it comes to agility, we can develop all the skills and put all the practices, processes, and organizational structures into place that we like, *but if we don't address mindset – individually and collectively – our change objectives and initiatives will fail or, at best, be short-lived.* If we don't get our individual mindsets right around agility, and embrace all the little knotty dilemmas and change signals that it naturally involves, we will struggle with the day-to-day challenges and choices that creating or participating in an agile organization inevitably requires.

Traditional *versus* agile mindset

While we have looked at some of the key psychological processes impacting our behavior and mindset at micro level, what do we actually mean by an agile mindset itself? Like agility, and indeed the Future of Work, mindset is a broadly used, yet poorly defined, term. Some consider it a state of mind, an orientation, a way of thinking, or mental attitude. Others refer to it as a combination of our intellectual, emotional, and physical states because the mind is a container for all three (thoughts, feeling, and expressed action).

In our context, and for the purpose of clarity, an agile mindset is the degree to which we are inclined toward "being" agile. It is not just about "doing" agile, in terms of adapting specific work practices and methods. It's about our genuine, deep-rooted conscious and subconscious disposition to seeing the world of work and learning in an open and evolving way.

An agile mindset is something like author Carol Dweck's "growth mindset" meets the *Agile Manifesto* with its principles such as outcome and customer focus, collaboration, iteration and experimentation. It infers a bias and orientation for purposeful action and an openness to change, learning, collaboration, iteration, diversity, and improvement.

To create a picture of the agile mindset, we all need our own reference points to visualize what we are aiming for, as well as an understanding of the traditional mindset it contrasts with. While each of us should create our own list of attributes based on our own experiences, **Table 3.1** might help.

Table 3.1: Traditional *versus* Agile Mindset

TRADITIONAL Mindset	AGILE Mindset
Past experience and knowledge determines future results (*Fixed Mindset*)	Thrives on challenge, continuous learning and new experience (*Growth Mindset*)
Manage change, minimize disruption	Embrace and be comfortable with change and ambiguity
Strategy, goals and objectives	Strategy exists to support a higher purpose and vision, stakeholder outcomes, and future possibilities
Action based on clear business case and evidence	Bias for informed action, iteration and experimentation
Work practices and processes focused on linear, prescribed and "waterfall" ways of working	Work practices focused on outcomes, values and principles – for example, iteration, adaptation, co-creation and "agile" ways of working
Emphasis on individual knowledge and expertise	Emphasis on collective knowledge, working in small teams and networks, collaboration, and diversity

As we know, the traditional attributes and qualities in the left column of the table are not "bad" and are frequently needed; we often require these attributes to help us focus and get things done. When faced with problems or tasks that are relatively straightforward, for example, more linear and "waterfall" ways of working are suitable to achieve a speedy and efficient outcome. However, the mindset features on the right are needed *more* when facing a complex, uncertain and continuously changing environment – which is an increasing reality in the changing world of work. It is just a simple fact that we will increasingly need to call on and develop such agile mindset attributes, habits and muscle memory in order to adapt and thrive into the future.

Almost all outstanding performers who have successfully adapted to significant change, in any walk of life, employed the mental and behavior attributes on the right side of **Table 3.1**.

Their stories are everywhere. A young woman I interviewed in my research for this book told me she was given the task of automating her own job! When I probed as to the possible career-limiting downsides of her assignment, she would have none of it. Her mindset was set on the growth opportunity that the experience offered. She saw it as a way to advance her understanding of how her field of work was changing. If her job was susceptible to automation, she wanted to be a part of it. She was determined to learn how to leverage her domain knowledge, combine it with what she was learning with new colleagues as part of the re-design and digitalization process, and to be even more relevant in her chosen field in the future. What's more, she was grateful to her company for involving her in the process and giving her to opportunity to grow and develop. She viewed it as an opportunity to future-proof her career. She knew automation in her field was inevitable; it was up to her to "lean in," take responsibility, and adapt to the situation. I left my discussion with this inspiring young woman convinced I had just witnessed the agile mindset in action and had met someone who was destined to thrive in the Future of Work.

Looking closer at her story, she was showing her capacity to access a growth and opportunity mindset to help her positively progress with optimism and purpose rather than get left behind. She demonstrated a "default" mindset that was naturally and instinctively oriented to adapting to their changing circumstances.

Having this agile mindset as our natural, habitual and instinctive "default" is required for Future of Work readiness and to help us thrive rather than just cope in the Future of Work. Having an agile mindset automatically will give us the open mindedness and space to consider the best course of action to take, to respond mindfully and deliberately and not just to react based on our traditional habits, patterns and norms.

Closing the knowing/doing gap

The adoption of the agile mindset may sound logical, appropriate, and attractive in theory and yet, there is often a gap between:

- What we might want or know to be true; and
- What we actually do.

Commonly referred to as the knowing/doing gap, popularized by Stanford professors, Jeffrey Pfeffer and Robert Sutton, and others, this gap is formed by all kinds of sub-conscious and deep-rooted assumptions, beliefs, habits, and behaviors.

If we sincerely believe the change we are looking for is in line with what we know is right for us, and we are willing to address the deep-rooted habits and behaviors that are getting in our way, then we can push through and close the knowing/doing gap and make the change happen. The challenge with adopting the agile mindset, therefore, is not just about intellectual and conscious logic; it's also about genuine *conviction* and a willingness to confront and overcome deep-rooted, often unconscious, beliefs, assumptions, and habits that have been built up over time. This is essentially the same process we talked about earlier in the context of brain science. A sense of commitment or urgency is necessary, along with the focus to push through the normal, mental agitation and initial resistance towards a goal or change state that we genuinely want to pursue.

How many times do we do things that we ought not do, but we do them anyway? How many times have we said, *"I know I need to lose weight. I must start that diet on Monday"*? The knowing/doing gap is something we've all experienced in many areas of our lives. That gap creates conflict between what we *should* and might like to do in a given situation, *versus* our actual our behavior, and the inevitable results of that behavior.

> **Having this agile mindset as our natural, habitual and instinctive "default" is required for Future of Work readiness and to help us to respond mindfully rather than simply to react.**

The primary source of this permanent battleground between what we know intellectually and what we actually do is our mindset at work. Acknowledge and tackle mindset, and we're on the track to success.

Canadian motivational coach and author, Bob Proctor, offers a helpful approach to the knowing/doing gap. He, like others, makes the distinction between the conscious and subconscious parts of our mind. While our conscious mind contains all the knowledge, is rational, and executes our decisions, the subconscious part of our mind is what *really* controls and determines our behaviors, our reactions, and importantly, our habits.

The subconscious controls the part of our minds that stores our own individual paradigms: repeated patterns of behavior that generate our day-to-day habits and routines. Organizational culture thought leaders, Gerry Johnson and Kevan Scholes, also position paradigm at the core of corporate culture, or "the way we do things around here." At the individual level, we are literally programmed from an early age and then further through our life experiences and environment. Countless little and large experiences contribute to the development of our paradigms and therefore our habits: our social and working environment, our upbringing, and even our DNA. Our habits are formed through repetition, and they determine our natural responses and our behavior. Understand our paradigm and habits, and we understand our mindset and we understand our results.

Take my dieting example. My conscious mind is full of all the right information. I have great data about what I should or should not eat: no problem there. I know the correct amount of carbs and protein, the whole routine. My rational, conscious mind thinks it is in the driver's seat with my eating decisions. But my subconscious mind has other ideas. It is wired from years of past habits and my paradigm says, "*It will be OK. Another piece of cake is fine. You deserve that second helping. You need a treat to lift your mood,*" and so on. The subconscious uses these ingrained thoughts to actively fight any new, troublesome, and uncomfortable thoughts of the conscious mind, which is trying in vain to restrain and take the healthy option.

We assume others have it cracked: they must have great discipline or better willpower than us. Not necessarily so. The people who appear to have it cracked simply have less of a gap between their conscious and subconscious minds, which are more aligned and in relative harmony. Perhaps their subconscious minds have been programmed from a very young age to instinctively recognize the benefits of restraint and healthy choices. They might not even know it, and have formed their healthy habits accordingly. Their knowing/doing gap is smaller than the gaping chasm others might have to confront as they approach the refrigerator or the cookie jar.

We have all seen the attempt to change in the workplace, too. An individual or a team tries to commit to a positive course of action only for it to fail at the first or second hurdle. The conscious mind says, *"Yes! Let's try this,"* but the subconscious mind ultimately says, *"No. It's too risky,"* or, *"Not today."* The new "thing" doesn't fit with the paradigm of what is comfortable and familiar. The dance of personal behavior and change has begun.

Think of the common activity of attending a training course. During the course, we're exposed to and convinced of the necessity for a new skill or habit change. We commit to doing things differently on Monday morning. (Why is Monday always the designated day?) We do it once, maybe twice, and then it's gone. The commitment and connection between the conscious and subconscious mind has not been made. The programming adjustment marked for change within our paradigm has only been made superficially, and it reverts back to type. Those fragile, neural pathways that were formed to move us in a positive behavioral direction have been beaten back by our old paradigm. Recall the neurochemical steps: *Focus, Act, Repeat, and Learn.* The subconscious mind has effectively delivered its verdict on the new idea or habit after allowing the conscious side to focus on it and play with it for a day or two. You can almost hear it say, *"Nah, not worth it. Stick with the tried and tested. It hasn't served you too badly up until now."* In the old world of work, we have been programmed and educated for clarity, rewarded and recognized according to traditional measures of success.

Now, in this new era of disruption, continuous change, and uncertainty, what does our subconscious mind want? Certainty, consistency with what we know, comfort, and clarity – words that don't sit well with the problems, choices, trade-offs, and solutions we face in the world of work and in our careers. As one program participant once told me: *"Agility makes my head hurt!"*

The agile mindset provides a mental model and a mechanism for paying attention to what is really going on between our good intentions, our conscious and subconscious mind, and our actual behaviors and outcomes. It helps us align all the elements at play – intellectual, emotional, and physical (think, feel, and act). Paying attention to our mindset gives us the space to stop and understand what we are doing and why, and whether we are moving in the right direction towards where we want to go, and who we want to be. Back to what Viktor Frankl said, *"Between stimulus and response there is a space. In that space is our power to choose our response."* We can use that space to steady ourselves and to push towards the change we want to see.

Re-programming our mindset

The good news is that if we become aware of what is really going on in our mind, we have the ability to determine our own outcomes: to essentially re-program our mindset if we want to do so – to be in control of this infinitely powerful resource rather than be the plaything of our emotional, reactive and sub-conscious selves. Wouldn't it be exhilarating and empowering to take more conscious control of closing our knowing/doing gap when it comes to our personal agility – and indeed other parts of our professional and personal lives? Wouldn't it be great if the more tricky and unconventional choices and decisions we know are right could be made a little more easily, rather than being trapped or cut off at the pass by our deep, hard-wired deference to convention, tradition, the *status quo*, and the more comfortable habits of the past?

We can! The science proves it, as do countless role models out there should we stop to observe them. And so it is with adopting an agile mindset. Here's some thoughts about how to get started.

Self-awareness

The first step in the agile mindset journey is self-awareness of what is going on in our conscious and subconscious minds, how we personally deal with change ourselves, and thinking about the future state we want to reach. With self-awareness and by making even small adjustments to close the gap, mindset can become our very best friend and ally rather than our saboteur-in-chief.

Honestly analyze which mindset attributes (traditional or agile) you most closely align with from **Table 3.2.** If your reflexes and subconscious habits more closely reflect those attributes on the right of the table, then you are in good shape to developing the processes, skills and practices that will deliver agility. If they are more to the left, celebrate those strengths but also reflect on how you might benefit from accessing the attributes of a more agile mindset in the future.

> **Mindset can become our very best friend and ally or our saboteur-in-chief.**

What habits do you currently engage in that are perhaps limiting your agility, and that might represent the dominance of a more traditional mindset? How could they (even one or two) be replaced with agile mindset habits that are more in line with where you want to go in the future?

At this point, we need to focus on and internalize the change we want to see, and why. Understanding our own purpose, our values, and what really drives us help us to visualize the personal benefits of making this effort and this shift. Such focus, desire, and commitment will strengthen those neural pathways, is necessary fuel for the personal change journey ahead, and helps us to be able to persist when difficulty arises. As Susan David points out in *Emotional Agility*, the power of "want to" goals is much greater than "have to" goals for sustainable outcomes and intrinsic motivation. If the shift towards more agile behavior feels like a chore that we should do simply because it is logical, we will likely fail when faced with big moments of choice. The benefits to us need to be emotional, not just rational.

And don't just do this self-reflection on your own – have some fun with it. Talk to others about how you and they typically manage change and react to changing circumstances. Observe and discuss it with others. As the famed psychologist and organizational expert, Elton Mayo, once said:

> ... *one friend, one person who is truly understanding, who takes the trouble to listen to us, can change our whole outlook on the world of work.*

Acceptance

After self-awareness comes acceptance. If we accept and embrace who and where we are, and where we have come from, then we can start to constructively explore and identify some of our individual blockers, habits, and behaviors.

Take a hard, honest look at your behavior and ask yourself: what are the comfortable and familiar habits that hold me back, that block my path towards a more open and agile outlook? Identify those (even just one or two at a time) and commit to replacing them with reinforcing habits and behaviors that are in line with where you want to go. Despite the self-talk your old paradigm will throw at you, your level of desire to change and your commitment ultimately will be what pushes you through.

Conscious programming

Being more self-aware and accepting of "triggering" thoughts and behaviors allows us to replace them with more enabling thoughts and ideas. Impressing, repeating and reinforcing positive thoughts and mental triggers will help us focus on, embrace and accept agility as good and normal. We then begin the process of reprogramming ourselves towards then benefits an agile mindset and the behavioral choices involved. Essentially, we are creating a new paradigm shift in our own mind, setting ourselves up for success.

With an eye on the goal, your subconscious mind will soon get the message that this change is for real and it might as well get on side. And, before you know it, you move from clunky, conscious incompetence in the new habit to unconscious competence, the knowing/doing gap is reduced or eliminated, and you have set a new base line for your future growth and improvement. And remember that you have been here before. Think about a change in your past that turned out better than you anticipated because of the actions you eventually took. Go back to your initial worries and concerns that never materialized (or at least not to the degree that you feared). What do you wish you had known then that you know now and how you would you advise someone else in the same situation?

Action and experimentation

Act! Change will not happen by thinking and reflecting alone. Action has to be taken as soon as the commitment to change is made. Take a single agility supporting practice that is meaningful to you and start with it. It will be awkward at first, but that is just the defensive norepinephrine in your brain doing its job. With the satisfaction that you are on the move and bolstered by some early, modest wins, the self-rewarding dopamine will soon kick in and you'll be on your way.

When these enabling and reinforcing habits become natural, the mind opens to the skills and practices that will continue to fuel the conscious mind to learn new enabling skills. It will make better decisions and choices than it did before, and the reinforcement cycle continues. You are in *Repeat & Learn* mode, and the cycle begins again with new situations and opportunities.

This is why the Agile People community and others place such stock on principles, such as psychological safety, experimentation, and servant leadership in creating agile work environments. These principles, amongst others, create the fertile conditions for continuous change and agility to prosper at individual, team, and ultimately, organizational levels.

Putting it all together

Figure 3.1 is a simple model that illustrates what might help you to make personal agility a personal habit.

Figure 3.1: The Agile Mindset in Action

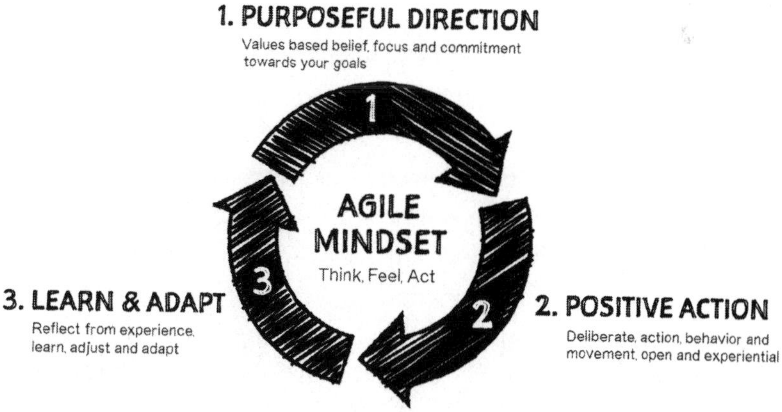

1. PURPOSEFUL DIRECTION
Values based belief, focus and commitment towards your goals

AGILE MINDSET
Think, Feel, Act

3. LEARN & ADAPT
Reflect from experience, learn, adjust and adapt

2. POSITIVE ACTION
Deliberate, action, behavior and movement, open and experiential

Underpinned by the strong, values-based purpose we want to see for the future, we commit and engage in positive intentional action, which we then learn from and iterate to help reinforce and inform our direction. This cycle allows us to stay focused on our own true north, while also focusing on short-term delivery, learning and adapting as we go.

At the core of this cycle, and masterminding its course, is an Agile mindset, which helps us to acknowledge, recognize, understand, and regulate our rational thoughts, emotional feelings, and our actions through our behavior. It ensures we maintain our resilience and ultimately create our own destiny as we navigate the Future of Work. This continuous, positive and purposeful reinforcement of our thoughts, feelings, and actions leads to more deliberate alignment between our conscious mind and sub-conscious mind and our subsequent behavior. Mastering the Agile mindset reminds us of the words of William Ernest Henley from his poem, *Invictus*:

> *I am the master of my fate. I am the captain of my soul.*

Where do we go from here?

Developing an agile mindset provides the basis for Future of Work readiness. It establishes a fertile ground for learning the skills necessary to execute good outcomes for our teams, our organizations, and ourselves. It helps us establish greater self-awareness and alignment between our physical, intellectual, and emotional states. If we do not attend to our mindset, our brains will find ways to sabotage our efforts, and we will not yield the sustainable results and adaptability we want for ourselves over time. Understanding mindset and the micro-change processes involved also helps us to be kinder to ourselves and others on this journey, as we all experiment with new skills and more agile ways of working compared to those we relied on in the past.

Having both an agile mindset and skillset is a powerful combination. Together, these competencies undoubtedly will enable every individual, employee, and leader to thrive in the Future of Work. The research, our own lived experiences, and the adaptive nature of the human race prove this to be the case. We just need to be more deliberate and conscious of this combination as a front-of-mind imperative. And we need to be better at teaching it to future generations so that they naturally adapt and thrive at a pace and frequency appropriate for the times. Building on the fertile ground of an agile mindset, and developing specific skills to achieve greater personal agility and adaptiveness is the subject of the next chapter.

What you can do
On the individual level:

- Think of any habit or skill you have successfully taken up or abolished in your life. It could be anything from driving, dieting to dancing! From what you have read in these pages, do you recognize the steps it took to successfully make that change?
- Using the steps in this chapter as a guide:
  - How does your mindset compare with the traditional *versus* agile mindset attributes?
  - What habits and behaviors are holding you back?
  - What one or two habits could you replace to improve your agile mindset?
  - What resources do you need or who could you talk to in order to understand more about your mindset and about how others adapt and change?
- Debate this issue with a colleague and get their perspective on your experiences and behaviors.

On the organizational level:

- Get working groups together to discuss what the agile mindset is, what it looks like, why it is important and what could be done at organizational level to help people develop it.

- Do leaders exhibit an agile mindset or a more traditional mindset? What could be done to support them develop an agile mindset both for themselves and to help them recognize and develop it in others?

- Do your organizational change management efforts take account of changing hearts as well as minds as part of the change process? Could more attention be given to the emotional side of managing change and in helping people engage their mindset towards the benefits of the change for them, as well as on the specific changes to their skills and their roles in the organization?

Chapter 4
THE AGILE SKILLSET

At the individual level, agility, along with resilience,
is the key adaptive quality required to deal with
increasing and turbulent change.
Joseph McCann & John Selsky

This quote from McCann and Selsky, and their accompanying research, make a strong case for the value of personal agility. But what are the specific, individual skills of agility that they and others are referring to as being critical for individuals to adapt to the jobs and careers of the future? In the last chapter, we looked at the role of mindset as a foundational factor in enabling individuals to thrive in the Future of Work. But mindset is not enough in itself. The right mindset needs to be fed with a skillset to fulfil its intent.

Being more deliberate and proactive in developing the skills (both hard and soft) needed for the future works, in tandem with an agile mindset, ensures an individual is equipped to succeed in an uncertain and rapidly changing work environment. More than any other time in history, we must understand and nurture the specific skills required to be adaptable, agile, and future-fit.

Adaptive skills and qualities for the Future of Work

Aside from an agile mindset and skillset, at a wider level what else does an individual employee or worker need to navigate and thrive in the Future of Work? What are the adaptive skills that will help people to future-proof their careers within a new employment relationship and talent management landscape? **Table 4.1** summarizes the findings from our field interviews, as well as the academic research on this question.

Table 4.1: Adaptive Qualities for a Future of Work Environment

THEME	ADAPTIVE QUALITIES
Digital leadership and mastery	o Awareness and openness to new technology both for the business (external perspective) and in terms of how work can be done differently within the organization using new technology
Networking and knowledge management	o The ability to manage and use networks inside and outside the organization o Collaboration and information management
Change openness and mindset	o Openness to change and volatility o Organizational capability to change rapidly and/or organically as needed
Career management and navigation	o Requirement on individuals to proactively manage their own careers and development o Organizational ability and willingness to facilitate learning needs of staff
Personal qualities and competencies	o Skills such as resilience, self-esteem, self-knowing and networking required to survive and adapt in a significantly new work and employment environment

The message from this research was clear. Underneath the more surface level vocational and ever changing technical skills required for Future of Work readiness, personal adaptiveness and agility came through as being core to an individual's enduring and ongoing ability to thrive and adapt to whatever circumstances and 'technical' skill requirements they will encounter in the Future of Work.

The benefits of improving personal agility go well beyond the impact to individuals themselves. For teams and organizations to be truly adaptive, future-fit, and agile, it follows that ultimately it is individuals within an organization who need to think, act, and perform in an agile way. What is culture, for example, but the repeated collective habits and behaviors of individuals who consciously (or subconsciously) choose to act one way or the other? However, in the rush towards top-down and corporate-driven transformation, we often underestimate the primacy of the individual when it comes to successful organizational change, organizational culture development, and organizational agility. It is the individual who is ultimately the source of organizational agility, not strategies, systems, tools or practices or even leaders.

Over the following pages we will explore the other side of the agile mindset/skillset coin – and focus on these more observable qualities associated with personal agility.

The Personal Agility Model

So, what does agility look like at the individual level – beyond surface level generalizations, inference, and guesswork? In this chapter, we turn our attention to these necessary behaviors and outline a framework that has practical applications for individual employees, and for business and HR leaders. The framework will be useful to business leaders in managing people and change in the workplace and to HR leaders in their recruitment, talent and development processes. It will also be useful to employees who want to remain relevant, fulfilled, and valuable in the Future of Work.

Fundamentally, personal agility refers to the qualities and attributes associated with agile performance and effectiveness at the *individual* level. The pace and scale of change in working life today suggests that there is value in identifying and developing these skills in a more conscious and front-of-mind way.

> **Ultimately it is individuals within an organization who need to think, act, and perform in an agile way.**

Our firm, WorkMatters, has developed a model summarizing these qualities, built from primary research and analysis of demonstrated and validated individual agile behavior and backed up by decades of academic research on workforce agility. The field research is validated through application and interviews with leaders and industry experts on organizational agility from around the world.

The questions behind the research were quite simple:

- What are the observable skills and behaviors of individuals who are clearly performing and thriving in fast-moving and changing work environments?
- What sets them apart from others?
- What do they do that leads to more positive outcomes and better results for themselves and for their teams?

These observed behaviors were analyzed and clustered into a number of themes or dimensions by their specific competencies. The qualities and attributes associated with individual agile performance and effectiveness are summarized in **Figure 4.1**, with the observable competencies most associated with each dimension outlined in **Table 4.2**.

Figure 4.1: The WorkMatters Personal Agility Model

Source: WorkMatters research.

Dimensions 1, 2, and 3 (Purposefulness, Learning Mindset, and Change Orientation) can be regarded as mainly individual, internal qualities or characteristics for which we have 100% control as individuals (*Personal Domain*).

Dimensions 4, 5, and 6 on the other hand (Autonomy & Empowerment, Relationship Management, and Collaborative) incorporate how an individual interacts with their work environment (*Social Domain*).

Table 4.2: The Dimensions and Competencies of Personal Agility

	DIMENSION	UNDERPINNING COMPETENCIES
Individual Domain	**Purposefulness:** An outlook and bias towards taking definitive action with the intent to achieve a particular outcome	o Self-led o Outcome-oriented o Aligned
	Learning Mindset: An orientation towards learning and an openness to connections, skills and perspectives outside one's own current frame of reference, knowledge and experience	o Systems thinking o Open o Learning-oriented o Resourceful o Learnability
	Change Orientation: The adaptive quality of being able to positively react and adapt to changes in the environment. Resilience describes the quality of being able to bounce back and to deal with the cognitive and physical challenges associated with change	o Adaptive o Resilient
Social Domain	**Empowered:** The extent of autonomy allowed or encouraged in taking action and decision-making within the workplace. Also includes the sense of confidence and willingness in an individual to embrace the empowerment offered or available	o Social empowerment o Self-empowerment
	Relationship Management: The ability to purposefully engage with and relate to others, to create networks and to build trust	o Networked o Impact and influence o Handles constructive conflict
	Collaborative: Includes the ability and orientation to work effectively within a team environment. It also explores the inclination to proactively invest in seeking and giving information	o Team-oriented o Knowledge-sharing

In looking at personal agility through these research-based dimensions, the model takes into account the environment in which employees work and interact, as well their own individual characteristics, qualities, and preferences. The observable competencies evident within each dimension were then identified, tested, and further expanded through more detailed descriptions and behavioral indicators.

Let's look a little closer at the six dimensions and competencies of personal agility.

1. Purposefulness

Purposefulness refers to an outlook, mindset, and bias towards taking definitive action with the intent to achieve a particular outcome. Underpinned by a core set of personal values and beliefs, there is strong sense of self-motivation and purpose in taking action towards outcomes for self, others, and/or the organization. In a work context, there is also the question of alignment between the organizational purpose, vision, and values and the extent to which these are connected to the individual's motivating purpose and values.

So much has been written about the impact and power of purpose, a topic that has only gathered pace over the last 20 years, or so. The American psychologist, Dr. Abraham Maslow, found that self-actualization and fulfillment was evident in those who had a sense of value and meaning in what they were doing.

In our own research, purpose was a quality abundantly evident in agile individuals. They were particularly clear on what they were about – and why. Not only did they have a strong sense of what they were aiming for in their work and how they did it, they also had a personal navigation system to get them back on track if and when they got rattled or knocked off-course. It was as if they had a compass or an internal rudder to keep themselves steady, and on-course towards where *they* wanted to go – not just where their manager or company wanted them to go. Self-leadership and self-motivation were evident in both their demeanor and their approach to work.

Having a sense of one's purpose helps to stabilize; to sustain focus and attention; to provide energy; and to trigger the right behaviors in challenging and rapidly changing circumstances. This inner clarity also provided strength and energy in the people we interviewed.

As Cathy Carlisi and her colleagues at the Boston Consulting Group point out:

> *Purpose is one of the most powerful intrinsic motivators because it speaks to both the head (as the compass that guides and aligns behaviors) and the heart.*

Jeroen Wels, EVP Human Resources at Unilever, also emphasizes the importance of purpose and "inner mobility:"

> *Future-fit skills are the currency that gets you meaningful experiences for a purposeful career. With Inner Mobility, we can further accelerate our transformation towards a more agile, innovative, and empowered organization.*

As with all the qualities represented in the Personal Agility Model, purposefulness is a learnable skill and an observable behavior – it can be worked at and developed. And along with Learning Mindset and Change Orientation, we found it to be a foundational skill that enabled other agility-oriented skills to emerge and prosper.

2. Learning Mindset
Learning mindset refers to a positive orientation towards learning and an openness to connections, skills, contradictions, and

perspectives outside one's own current frame of reference, knowledge, and experience. This dimension was possibly the most common area cited in our research.

The importance of having a learning mindset to adapt to changing circumstances is well documented. According to Starkey, Tempest & McKinlay in *How Organizations Learn*, learning orientation is a strategic necessity to:

> ... *promote individual self-development within a continuously self-transforming organization.*

Carol Dweck's "growth mindset" approach, Kryscynski, Brockbank & Ulrich's concept of "navigating paradox," introduced in *Victory Through Organization*, and Peter Senge's five disciplines – systems thinking, mental models, personal mastery, building shared vision and team learning – all provide useful adaptive learning concepts that are highly relevant in the context of developing personal and organizational agility.

3. Change Orientation

Change orientation refers to being able to positively react and adapt to changes in the work environment. An individual's ability to react and change, as well as his or her capability to recognize and embrace the benefits of change, are two key aspects of personal agility.

Orienting to change is an increasingly necessary element of modern organizational culture and new ways of working. Employers are also paying more attention to the qualities associated with "change-able" employees, such as being open, flexible, engaged, and ultimately, energized and motivated towards growth and new ideas.

Change orientation needs to include coping skills and mechanisms for it to be a sustainable and positive experience for growth and performance.

Two key elements or competencies associated with personal agility are:

- **Adaptiveness:** The ability to reinvent and grow; and
- **Resilience:** The ability to bounce back and deal with adversity.

In order to perform in organizations where, as McCann & Selsky put it, "the pace and disruptiveness of change is relentless," individuals need a combination of the two.

> **It is the individual who is ultimately the source of organizational agility.**

These skills come from deep within us. They are developed over time and through individual life experience. While undoubtedly learned, they are seldom, if ever, taught in any deliberate way throughout childhood or early adult life. We are conditioned, trained and developed for a more "certain, plan and controlled" existence, an aspect of our education system that must surely be challenged more in the future. As we explored through neuroscience in **Chapter 3**, we are also naturally wired to essentially resist change. And, despite the pace and complexity of our 21st century world, our legacy 20th century educational and business models can approach change as something to be minimized and controlled.

Resilience and agility are essentially joined at the hip. Resilience is that gritty ability to absorb disruption and persist in difficult circumstances. Agility, on the other hand, is about sensing and responding to a change or situation, or to what is going on in the wider environment. It is a more positive, forward-looking capability where there is sense of movement and progression towards a better outcome. If resilience is about surviving, agility is about thriving.

The personal mental challenges encountered with continuous change also need to be acknowledged, and they highlight the importance of resilience, and indeed purposefulness, so that change is a sustainable and bearable "habit" over time. Resilience is gaining more attention, in its own right, in the management of the health and well-being as well as organizational agility and performance.

John Herlihy, ex-VP of Google and ex-VP, EMEA and LATAM at LinkedIn, stresses the importance of resilience in dealing with rapidly changing work environments:

Resilience is a real skill and quality that needs more active attention in our education system and early work experiences today – it is a quality that will be deliberately sought in future hiring and promotion decisions as change continues to be a more constant fact of working life than ever before.

4. Autonomy and Empowerment

Autonomy and empowerment was another common theme in our research: a sense of autonomy and empowerment was key to self-direction and adaptiveness. Ultimately, people only do what they believe, and they only believe what they discover for themselves.

In the work context, empowerment refers to the extent of autonomy within the workplace, which means that people are encouraged to take action and make decisions. The changing nature of the workplace, along with the uncertainties it brings, demands independent, creative, competent, and empowered employees. From the employee perspective, empowerment contributes to job satisfaction, creativity, intrinsic motivation, performance, and organization commitment.

However, empowerment is a two-way street. As important as it is to have an environment that is conducive to creating empowerment, employees must also want to be empowered in the first place. This capacity to individually accept, seek and embrace empowerment should not be underestimated.

Psychological empowerment is defined by Professor Scott Seibert and others as an individual's "intrinsic task motivation reflecting a sense of self-control in relation to one's work and an active involvement with one's work role." The key message is that empowerment is not just a condition of the work environment provided, or not, by management for others to be empowered (*social empowerment*) – it is an active, self-starting, learnable skill that needs to be sought and created and pursued at individual level, as well (*self-empowerment*).

In our research, the skill of self-empowerment and self-leadership was a standout difference between people who were visibly agile and those who were happy to just go with the flow and work reactively, usually under clear direction from others or from precedence. This latter group, as pointed out by McCann & Selsky, then struggled when confronted by significant change and turbulence. Managing empowerment and autonomy is, therefore, an important task of leaders. They need to address the sense of confidence, psychological safety, and motivation an employee feels when taking on delegated tasks and growing through operational accountability.

When speaking about the importance of genuine empowerment during the implementation of Honeywell Global's *Connected Workplace Strategy*, the company's Real Estate Director said:

> *Creating a workplace environment that places people in the*
> *center of its design means empowering employees to have a say,*
> *giving them ample opportunity to understand and ask questions.*

This allows us to constantly shift, and we have people at each location able to help implement change and keep staff engaged with that change.

5. Relationship Management

Relationship management and how we "show up" in our relationships was an important factor in effective personal agility from our research. In a rapidly-changing world of work, we do not individually have all the knowledge needed to solve interconnected and complex situations. We need others to fill in the gaps and help us solve increasingly complex problems at pace – and they need us too.

From a skills-based perspective, we found that relationship management specifically involved the ability to purposefully engage with and relate to others, to create networks, and to build trust. Rising above personal preferences in order to see the bigger picture, it also includes the ability to embrace constructive conflict with direct and open dialogue, which demonstrates interpersonal impact and influence to ultimately achieve superior team learning and outcomes.

At the base of any strong and sustainable relationship is trust, which emerged from the WorkMatters research as a critical factor for individuals to work in a genuinely collaborative and psychologically safe way. The literature also confirms a significant direct link between organizational trust and organizational agility. This makes sense when you consider that change requires trust, particularly when our information may not always be clear or complete. People must trust in the direction they are going and in who is doing the asking. Are those with whom I am collaborating trustworthy and do they have my back? Can I be candid? Will my feedback be given and taken in the spirit of learning, growth, and improvement, rather than met with resentment or defensiveness? These are basic human needs in any relationship that, with skill and deliberate action, we can impact and develop.

If resilience is about surviving, agility is about thriving.

An example of a company that has deliberately worked to create an environment of trust to support an agile skillset is Deloitte. The firm developed a culture where output matters more than "presenteeism," and where employees feel trusted to work in a way that suits both them and the business. Working was based on three principles:

- Outcomes (not inputs);
- Mutual trust; and
- Two-way open communication.

Deloitte's Head of Client Service HR, Caroline Hunt, said:

> *It's about give and take, starting with the principle of mutual trust and that people are accountable for their role in delivering the best service to their clients.*

Since the future workplace will increasingly require the development of cross-cultural teams across different countries, more remote working and working within increasingly diverse workforces, employees must develop good relationship and conflict management skills to succeed, innovate, and thrive. It was evident from our research that such skills came quite naturally to agile individuals. The purpose behind any exchange was always clear. There was a positive intent and openness to both giving and receiving feedback towards the achievement of positive, shared outcomes.

A final element identified in the effective relationship management skills of agile individuals was the development and cultivation of networks. Proactive and constructive development of networks contributed to both personal and organizational agility. At the organizational level, the cumulative or compound power of networks and linkages (based on social capital theory) lead to enhanced intellectual capital and knowledge management effectiveness in the organization, which can in turn improve a firm's competitive advantage.

6. Collaborative

Collaboration is closely related to relationship management but it specifically includes the ability and orientation to work effectively within a team environment. It emerged from the research as an independent variable. The collaboration skillset also included the inclination to proactively seek and give information and insight to achieve superior outcomes than is possible when working on one's own.

The importance of effective teamwork and collaboration for organizational agility is prominent in the literature and in practice. Teams are the basic unit for task completion in an agile organization and are only as good as the individuals within them. Information exchange is essential to effectively manage change in organizations and to produce effective team units.

In a McKinsey study, nearly 80% of the senior executives surveyed highlighted that effective collaboration management:

> ... across product, functional, and geographic lines was essential for growth,

yet only 25%:

> ... described their organizations as "effective" at sharing knowledge across internal and external boundaries.

A striking finding from the research was the emphasis interviewees again placed on trust in creating the circumstances for optimal collaboration and a true learning environment.

Personal agility assessment

The Personal Agility Model outlined above has been further developed as an online, self-assessment questionnaire, and 360-degree tool for individual development and growth. Created and validated in partnership with Trinity College Dublin, it provides individuals with valuable insight into:

- How they can improve their own personal agility today;
- How they can build their personal resilience, adaptiveness, and "career-fitness" into the future.

The full version of the Personal Agility Assessment consists of 57 statements covering the six dimensions and 17 individual competencies described above and listed in **Table 4.2**, with output and feedback similar to that in **Figure 4.2**.

Figure 4.2: The Personal Agility Radar

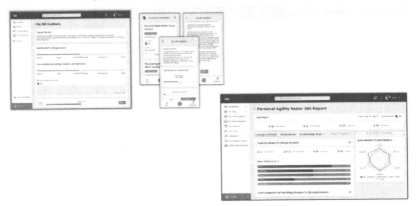

For employees, it provides a summary of the skills they need to thrive in an agile work environment in a sustainable way and future-proof their careers as circumstances change. The tool facilitates a growth-oriented process of self-reflection and feedback on an employee's strengths and possible development areas when it comes to these adaptive and Future of Work oriented skills.

For organizations, the assessment clarifies the skillset of the "Agile employee" and facilitates the effective recruitment and development of such skills. It summarizes the skillset of prospective, future-fit employees that business and HR leaders need to consider if they are to source, develop, and retain the workforce and talent they will need to future-proof their organizations.

Being able to identify and measure personal agility is an important step, but even more important is to establish ways to nourish and develop these skills for the benefit of both the organization and the employee. Employers, therefore, need to incorporate these qualities into their selection, promotion, and recruitment processes. Leadership development needs to include awareness of these adaptive skills so that leaders know how to recognize, coach, and develop them in their teams, as well as in themselves.

Embedding awareness of and focus on these personal agility skills into the talent management, personal development, and leadership development infrastructure of an organization will help to ensure that people are armed with the skills to help them thrive where they are today and be able to adapt into the future, either inside or outside their current employer.

Where do we go from here?

The six dimensions of personal agility introduced in this chapter – Purposefulness; Learning Mindset; Change Orientation; Autonomy and Empowerment; Relationship Management; and Collaborative – demonstrate the need to focus on the human aspects of agility to achieve the ultimate goal of organizational agility. These six dimensions also play a crucial role in helping people to shape their own personal Future of Work. It follows that employees, employers, and educators need to incorporate such personal agility competencies into their recruitment processes as well as learning and development strategies.

These competencies could be summarized into a definition for personal agility:

> *The capability to sense, respond, and adapt to changing circumstances applying purpose, openness and resilience in learning new skills, developing new solutions, and delivering positive outcomes with and through others.*

A bit of a mouthful perhaps but, on inspection, a useful summary of the key ingredients of personal agility and individual preparedness for the Future of Work. Going back to the foundational power and impact of mindset in **Chapter 3**, we can, with repetition and experimentation, impress on both our conscious and subconscious minds the importance of developing this skillset and our intention to prioritize these skills for continuous growth and experimentation into the future.

Increasing awareness, measurement, and development of these skills will help employees and employers alike to identify, develop and manage personal agility in a more deliberate way, resulting in more future-fit and agile individuals, teams, and organizations. The Personal Agility Model and Assessment is just one mechanism that can help surface these skills in a more proactive way than ever before.

With a greater understanding of the agile mindset and skillset at the individual level, it is easier to put the talent, leadership, and HR agenda, their consequences and their implications into context when it comes to creating and enabling organizational agility. We will explore how the agile mindset and skillset continue to emerge as key factors for talent, leaders, and HR when considering Future of Work readiness in **Part Three.**

What you can do
On the individual level:

- Consider the following questions and assess your own Future of Work readiness with regard to personal agility:

  o How resilient are you to change? From examples in your past, what tools have you experienced or seen that will help you improve your resilience in the future?

  o In reviewing the six key dimensions and 17 individual competencies in the Personal Agility Model in **Table 4.2**, how would you rate yourself from 1 to 10? What would be your priority dimensions for future development?

  o What plan do you have to further develop the dimensions you may want to work on?

  o Within both the individual and social domains, what specific action have you taken, or do you intend to take, to learn more and be open to other possibilities?

On the organizational level:

- How do the skills of personal agility "show up" in your key talent management and HR processes – for example, recruitment, assessment, training and development, performance management, promotion, succession planning etc.?

- How do you, or could you, deliberately develop these skills in employees through:

  o Formal training;

  o Focused work experience;

  o Mentoring and coaching from managers?

- How do leaders and managers rate when it comes to their own personal agility and how can they be supported in recognizing and developing these skills in others?

Part Three

SHAPING THE FUTURE READY ORGANIZATION

Chapter 5

A NEW EMPLOYMENT DEAL FOR THE FUTURE OF WORK

There has never been a better time and there has never been a more concerning time for employees today.
Erik Brynjolfsson & Andrew McAfee

This quote from Brynjolfsson & McAfee, introduced earlier in **Chapter 1**, captures the new landscape of work and employment today. Their observation highlights the dilemma for current and prospective employees facing the Future of Work. There has never been a better time to be an employee with special skills or the right education because these people can use technology to create and capture value. However, there's never been a more precarious or concerning time to be an employee with "ordinary" skills because computers, robots, and other digital technologies are replacing those same skills at an extraordinary rate.

The paradox is also noted by futurist and author, Martin Ford, in his book, *The Rise of the Robots*, who argues that:

> *... workers will face an unprecedented challenge as they attempt to adapt.*

So what are the implications of the new world of work and increased organizational agility for the employee of the future?

What will the new talent landscape look like, and what will be different than the traditional employment models of the past? Having looked closely at the Future of Work implications for the individual in **Chapters 3** and **4**, this chapter seeks to explore the wider talent agenda as it relates to future-based organizational trends and global workplace realities.

A mindset shift is required not just on the part of individuals, but also amongst employers, educators, policy-makers, and by society at large regarding traditional assumptions about employment and jobs in the Future of Work. Being aware of what's ahead will help people proactively navigate the new talent landscape in a more conscious, confident and deliberate way, rather than just reacting to an ever-shortening and continuously changing lifecycle for skills and talent.

A tipping point for the world of work?

In the advent of Future of Work trends – more widespread acceptance of remote working, enabled technology, and an insatiable need in the market for specific skills on demand – the knowledge worker's future seems bright; even more so if they employ an agile mindset and keep their skills up-to-date, as set out in **Chapters 3** and **4**. On the other hand, the digital divide, automation, and the precarious nature of work suggest there will be challenges ahead. Many experts and observers continue to address, predict, and debate this unfolding scenario.

Jeanne Meister and Karie Willyerd, in *The 2020 Workplace*, warn about the risk of being "left behind" as the knowledge economy and the race for highly-skilled talent increases at the expense of more routine and lower-skilled workforce. A clear challenge exists for employees with skills whose jobs and livelihoods are at risk from automation and redundancy. While optimists correctly talk about the creation of new jobs as technology augments and upgrades the quality and productivity of human work rather than replacing it, we need also to acknowledge that jobs are being – and will continue to be – under threat, hollowed out, and lost. We need to properly understand the skills needs for the replacement jobs of the future so that, with better planning and preparation, these jobs are not out of reach for an unprepared, unskilled or semi-skilled workforce.

There are many warning signs that trouble may lie ahead but it's not all bad news. More jobs will be inevitably created in the current Fourth Industrial Revolution and demand for basic services is evolving, changing, and even holding its own against the threat of automation and digitalization. For those with access to decent education, most of the challenges that individuals face in the Future of Work are within their control through increased awareness and learning – if they are open to adapting, upskilling, and re-booting based on the evolving demands and opportunities for human labor, talent, and skills. With the advancement of the Internet age, learning and skills development options have been increasingly democratized for those who can access such tools and resources.

The core necessity for digital literacy has already taken hold throughout the workplace. It will only continue to increase as organizations invest further in digital platforms and technology to remain competitive and responsive in the future market. Those who are open to mastering new skills will thrive and remain relevant for the evolving opportunities of the future. Those who ignore the trends, or who lack access to such learning and development skills, will not.

Many organizations are aware of this skills agenda and are proactively actively upskilling their employees for the digital world. I share just a few key initiatives from global brands here:

- Back as far as 2009, Ford launched its Digital Worker Program in the UK to help staff more flexibly integrate to a more global, connected, and mobile workforce. Benefits of the program included clear increases in personal and team productivity and engagement. Mark Ovenden, former President of Ford Motor International Markets, said:

    The program has enabled our employees to better balance their work and home lives and helped them to work more effectively in a global business across different continents and time zones. The economic climate has emphasized the importance of these Agile working practices and demonstrated that they can offer organizations a win-win competitive advantage with our employees.

- As part of its mobile working/location-independent working program, the BMW group offered its employees a wide range of flexible modules so they can tailor when and where they work to their personal needs, enabling agile working and an optimal work-life balance;

- At IBM Greenock, Scotland, identification of changing markets and the commoditization of hardware moving East led to building a strategic roadmap of opportunities for a new, sustainable mission in support of IBM's global strategy. IBM Greenock embarked on an employee up-skilling program, which was considered critical since the future success of the operation and the viability of the workforce was dependent on the innovation and upskilling of the employees to move up the value chain. The program resulted in employees who previously worked in lower-skilled roles moving to working and developing higher value solutions for global clients;

- Guardian Insurance had its administration teams have "play dates" with robots within their teams in advance of their inevitable introduction. The goal was to get staff used to the technology and to contribute to what it could and could not do for the customer before adapting their jobs and working with this emerging technology, rather than feeling threatened of being replaced by them.

As significant and innovative as such solutions are, the challenges (and opportunities) associated with the new world of work is not just about skills alone. Broad-based employment longevity and viability in the global world of work are also reliant on *how* those skills are accessed and utilized by the widest possible population.

Since the beginning of the 21st century, work has become a more fragmented, temporary, and precarious thing. We have seen the increased global fragility in labor and employment. How this has played out in the societal and political landscapes as a result has been plain for all to see. In a competitive global economy, employers are seeking optimum flexibility in how, where, when, and by whom work gets done and how labor is contracted. Advancements in technology and other pressures are resulting in an increasing array of options that are now open to employers as to how work gets done. This, in turn, is generating increasing numbers of different "worker types," from traditional employees to contractors to gig workers.

A fluid supply and demand model for skills and services is totally disrupting the traditional "20th century" employer/ employee relationship. Agency and gig working continues to grow as a strong percentage of the total workforce. Business models like Airbnb demonstrate the new, technology-enabled ways services are delivered by a global "workforce" of property owners. Yet, growing pains in organizations that depend on Uber-type "employment" approaches continue to be felt. And propelled by the pandemic and other disruptions, organizations are re-engineering their work design models and working arrangements to accommodate new ways of getting work done by those who work directly and indirectly for them.

It is clear that the traditional 20th century employment deal needs a fundamental re-set.

For those in direct employment, the picture is also not as secure as perhaps it used to be. The lack of security is demonstrated by the continuous lurches back and forth of employment and unemployment data. No matter how progressive or well-meaning an employer makes its environment or brand, ultimately (and inevitably), the workforce is on the precarious side of every financial indicator a business turns to when the going gets tough. Dr. Jean Cushen of Maynooth University conducted research into the employer/employee relationship over the last 10 years and observed:

> ... whether based on any return on capital or cost-oriented metric, labor is always on the losing side.

While many organizations will argue that this blunt view of the employer/employee relationship is not applicable in their case, the fact is that, over the past 20 years, employer-sponsored jobs, financial security, and stability have eroded – and both parties know it.

The old deal is dead

Against the backdrop of the rapidly-evolving employment and labor market realities, it is clear that the traditional 20th century employment deal has been eroding for decades and is fundamentally dead. At the very least, it is in need of a fundamental and unambiguous re-set.

The message to employees and other worker types is that they must take more direct responsibility for their own future. This imperative was made clear during the financial crisis, when employees around the world were laid off by the millions and with astonishing haste. I recall when, as part of my own work, researching and discussing the "engagement and employment challenge," employees would say, *"I now realize that I can't rely on my employer for my future financial or career security. At least, in the future, give me the opportunity and support to future-proof my own financial and career path."* As a direct consequence of employee sentiment during this time, trust and confidence in employers sank to an all-time low. Loyalty cuts both ways. One could argue that employers' deep and harsh reaction to the financial crisis, with so many people suffering the brunt of the accountant's pen, had a bearing on the political, populist, and societal trends of the decade that followed.

During the early months of the COVID-19 crisis, there seemed to be an awareness of the cost of the previous "cut deep and fast" approach that occurred during the financial crisis. Governments and employers intervened and invested faster and deeper to protect employees from the initial stages of the pandemic. Was the contrasting response due to the differences between a financial crisis and a health and human crisis? Or perhaps it was just easier to access capital for what was hoped to be a temporary crisis? Has the increased attention from the boardroom and investment community – through more socially conscious investment models like environmental, social and governance (ESG) investment standards) – influenced a more balanced, rather than a primarily financial, approach to dealing with an employment crisis and labor market policy in general? Time will tell.

The bottom line is that, with a little over 20% of the 21st century gone, two global disruptions to the world of work occurred with many other mini-shocks at country, sectoral, and company levels.

More disruption undoubtedly will come in the future. In parallel, meanwhile, the unstoppable trends of enabling technology, climate change, and increased complexity in a globally interconnected marketplace, ever-changing consumer demand and expectations, and the increasing pace of change continue unabated.

If all these factors taken together do not constitute a paradigm shift in the world of work, I don't know what does. Leaders, citizens, educators, and policy-makers simply need to be clearer and more up-front about these shifts. In so doing, we can start to join policy and practice to enable both employers and employees to adapt and thrive within a "new employment proposition" for the future. But what does the future hold, in practical terms, for employers and employees?

The employer perspective

The organization of the future will need to be an increasingly agile and responsive entity, able to adapt to change coming from many directions whether technological, consumer-driven, or environmental. To survive – let alone thrive – an employer has little choice but to seek flexibility and creativity in its most important competitive advantage: its people.

The talent challenges for employers of the future will be about "accessing" skills from anywhere, at any time, at the right price, rather than "owning" those skills through the traditional, full-time employment model. Employers will need to direct this talent towards goals and priorities that are likely to shift and change faster than in previous generations.

The modern organization walks a delicate line between, on the one hand, wanting loyalty, commitment, and longevity from its workforce while, on the other hand, needing flexibility and leaving open the possibility of parting ways when things change.

Employers are seeking maximum engagement, creativity, innovation, and commitment without necessarily being able to provide the desired security and loyalty in return.

This reality must be considered hand-in-hand with the Future of Work, and factored into how individuals can be supported, under our duty of care as employers, to build sustainable skills and fulfilling careers, while also developing flexibility, agility, and change-ability into our organizations. Our 20th century employment models are not built for a more dynamic 21st century employer/employee relationship.

The employee perspective

From an employee perspective, the precarious reality of modern working life lives side-by-side with a world of work that has vast opportunity and potential. The changing world of work has a bright side and a shadow side.

For many employees, particularly the average knowledge worker, access to a global reservoir of knowledge and skills has never been easier or cheaper. For others, the world of work has become more challenging, volatile, and inaccessible. The digital divide, inequity, and changing consumer habits and behaviors have put many lower-skilled and lower-paid workers at risk of being left behind. And there is the danger that both the digital and income divide could get even wider in the coming years.

As we know from our research, employees want purpose and growth; they want to contribute and they want satisfaction from their work. Are these aims reconcilable with employer's ultimate need to be flexible and agile?

The employee perspective is therefore a paradoxical one, much like that of the employer. While job security and purposeful attachment to a particular employer may be the ideal, the relationship could turn sour at any point. Gone are the days of the

40-year pension plan, which is precisely why employees need an agile mindset and a skillset in pursuit of their own longer-term career goals so they can continue to adapt and thrive either inside or outside a specific organization.

In the fragmented and precarious employment environment of the future, pay, pensions, and tenure are not as secure and predictable as they once were. Traditional education can't keep pace with changing skills needs, and the responsibility for securing a progressive working future shifts to the employee to a greater extent than ever before. The employee needs to take control of his or her own career and financial security.

A new social contract is needed that clarifies the expectations and responsibilities of all actors in the employment relationship.

Given these contrasting forces at play in the modern employment deal on both sides, a more mature and open employment relationship and conversation is therefore needed across the board.

The best employers will demonstrate their "duty of care" in new ways. They will consciously develop their employment brands to attract and retain the best – while also investing in helping employees to future-proof their skills and careers, whether they stay with the organization or not.

Policy-makers must also reimagine and adapt educational, social security and work activation models to reflect the new labor market and employment realities. In essence, a new "social contract" is needed to clarify the expectations and responsibilities of the different actors in the employment relationship, including employees and job seekers themselves. This is a big switch from a guaranteed steady career track with reliable income, or from the state picking up the pieces every time there is an inevitable turn or disruption at company, industry or economy level.

The new deal

Amid all the changes and contradictions in the new world of work, the employer/employee relationship is finding a new expression. It must, because it can never go back to what it was, and choices need to be made about what it looks like in the future. The pendulum may be swinging towards a different form of commitment between employer and employee; there is a "new deal" on the horizon, with some interesting elements at play.

While adaptability and resilience are more important than ever before for employers, purpose, meaning, flexibility, and opportunities for learning are growing in importance and relevance for employees. An increasingly important consideration for employers is the sustainability agenda. This includes an emerging imperative and trend towards developing a progressive employment proposition for the employee of the future. Developing and meeting ESG standards will require, or at least urge, employers to commit to progressive labor practices, upskilling employees, and generally mitigating against the precarious and volatile nature of work that is so vividly apparent in this century to date.

At the heart of the new deal is a simple, honest, adult-to-adult and authentic dialogue between employer and employee. Rosabeth Moss Kanter noted such dialogue 20 years ago in her book, *Evolve!*, when the need for a re-set of the employment relationship first started to emerge. Kanter talked about a "renewable commitment," where employers offer employees continuous development and job enrichment but without the pretense (on either side) of a job for life. Based on its research into the employment deal for the Future of Work, Accenture also talks about the ambition for every worker to be "net better off" as a result of their experience with their employer. The concept of "net better off" is measured across a range of criteria, including financial, well-being, relational, employability and purposeful.

Mihaly Nagy, Founder and CEO of the HR Congress and The HR Congress Summit Series has observed this gradual evolution of the employee deal over the years and what is yet to come.

> *We have successfully moved the needle from 'employee satisfaction to 'engagement' and now more fashionably 'employee experience' – and I see the next phase as one of ' people meaning and abundance,' where we shall be creating humane and people-centric workplaces not just because it makes business sense but because it makes human sense.*

Table 5.1: Old Deal *versus* New Deal

OLD DEAL focus	NEW DEAL focus
Contract focused on terms around the role and conditions	Agreement based on growth and an honest and transparent "renewable commitment"
Employer-centric	Two-way
Attraction to role and offer	Attraction to organizational purpose and growth potential
Employer-to-employee relationship	Adult-to-adult relationship
Duration and role with this employer	Sustainability and growth of the individual with the employer or beyond
Relatively fixed terms, conditions, and working arrangements	Optimum flexibility in the full employment offering and working arrangements
Directive relationship	Facilitative relationship
Train for competence for the job	Train for skills for the job and beyond

This new, more enlightened phase of work is undoubtedly underway and will be underpinned by some basic guiding principles as outlined in **Table 5.1**.

The new deal has begun and will continue to find its way into the more formal employment propositions and policies offered by employers. Mercer, the global human resources and benefits consulting firm, captures the basic essence of this emerging new deal (**Figure 5.1**). The model conveys the combination of the contractual, experiential and more inspirational aspects of what an employer must offer to attract and retain talent in the new world of work.

Figure 5.1: The Mercer Employee Proposition Model

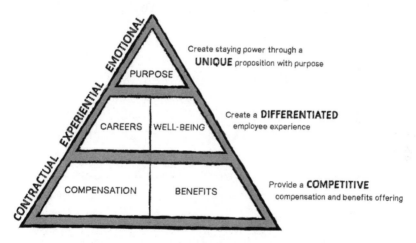

Changes are afoot in corporate land

In the corporate world, there is growing evidence that progressive organizations are leading the way by embracing the challenges of this new employment deal and helping to future-proof their workforces. For example, within the Business In The Community Group in Ireland, the CEOs of the country's leading employers formed a number of taskforces to progress priority areas of employment and environmental sustainability. As an invited member of the "Worker of the Future" taskforce, I saw first-hand the genuine care and commitment demonstrated by some organizations to develop practical solutions and future-proof Ireland's workforce.

> **Gone are the days of the 40-year pension plan. A new deal is underway in the world of work.**

There are a growing number of examples internationally of individual companies making an effort to embrace a more informed and progressive employment deal with employees. Ultimately, their goal is to help create agility and sustainability at both the company and individual level. Here are just a few cases:

- To help Novartis fulfill its purpose of reimagining medicine, the company embarked on a global initiative to unleash the talent, engagement, and creativity of its people. Through activities such as purpose workshops, performance management reform, overhauling of well-being, learning and leave programs (including digital awareness programs), the revamp of its purpose-driven employee proposition saw an 88% increase in hires made *via* Glassdoor and a 72% increase through LinkedIn;

- Dan Schulman, President and CEO at PayPal, an advocate of moral leadership who notably says that *"Capitalism is in need of an upgrade,"* spearheaded a number of ground breaking initiatives at the company, including the introduction of a new employee-centric approach to manage employee compensation. PayPal's Net Disposable Income approach recognizes the limitations of market-based pay systems and norms and seeks to create a fair, individual, and sustainable pay model for all employees;

- Staying with the idea of net value to the employee, as mentioned earlier, Accenture conducted research into how employers are helping their employees to be "net better off" through a combination of financial, well-being, relational, purpose-oriented, and employable "benefits" or dimensions at work;

- International household products manufacturer, WD-40, led by CEO Garry Ridge, is passionate about its purpose-driven employee-centric culture and inclusive "tribal" employment proposition. Its focus on community and cultural attributes such as values, knowledge, celebration, ceremony, and a strong sense of belonging is geared towards creating a self-sustaining work environment where people genuinely want to stay and grow.

Such practices and trends amongst large corporates are important to shine a light on what is emerging in the changing world of work. These examples demonstrate how employers are increasingly acknowledging their employees as central stakeholders in the future of their business models and not just as an operational necessity. It is refreshing to see large employers recognize their duty of care to the future development, sustainability and future-proofing of their workforces. Perhaps it would be cheaper and quicker to simply pay and develop their employees just enough so that they are optimizing their "human resources" to deliver value over the short term. Yet, these organizations understand that long-term success (for themselves and for the employees) ultimately depends on the innovation, commitment, agility, and skill of the workforce to pivot when disruption strikes.

Case in Point 5.1: Menlo Innovations

Background

Menlo Innovations is a software design company and an example of a firm basing the business model on the primacy of its people and team collaboration. To help achieve this, the company aims to incorporate "joy" to all stakeholders: the end users, the clients, and employees.

Key Take-aways

o Teams ("high-tech anthropologists") are sent out to observe, listen, and understand the nuanced needs of the end user.

o Project managers keep clients up-to-date with weekly "show and tells," transparency with project completion, and financials.

o The team works on an open floor plan, uses visual methods and tools to prioritize tasks

o Strong emphasis on experimentation, flexibility, and innovation to deliver results.

o Work/life balance is also emphasized, with all employees working *only* 40 hours and a strict no overtime/weekend work policy.

o The large team is broken down into teams of two, tasked with taking up projects that are of particular interest and motivating. Each team of two has only one monitor and one keyboard. Menlo has found this is the quickest way to share knowledge among the larger team, break down knowledge silos, and onboard people.

o The hiring interview includes the interviewee being paired with a member of the team to work on a project. Selection is based on whether the team felt the interviewee could convince them to hire his/her partner.

o The team as a whole makes performance reviews and personnel decisions.

Sources

https://menloinnovations.com/our-way/our-people

In recent years, it has been even more inspiring to note the growing number of purpose-led smaller organizations leading by example in shaping the Future of Work. Principles of workforce centricity, people commitment, growth and duty of care are apparent from day one of their existence – as part of their overall business model, employee proposition, and culture. In the early stages of a company's formation – start-up and scaling – when resources, budgets, and leadership time are scarce, it is easy for such enterprises to default to traditional, cost-driven employment mindsets. It is surely tempting to revert to the old "tried and true" employment methods, especially when it comes to matters of employee reward, development, and long-term sustainability. However, "new age" organizations such as Viisi, Menlo, Buurtzorg and BuJo highlighted in this chapter and elsewhere in the book as cases in point, chose to think differently. In doing so, they have demonstrated what a different employment deal can look like in the 21st century world of work.

While every organization's own experience and ambition will differ, the direction of travel is towards more purpose-driven, agile, "mature," and employee-centric work models that make sense for them and their workforces. The growing commitment in larger organizations to elements of the new, more sustainable employment deal, and the growing evidence of these principles at play in start-ups all over the world, provides some encouraging signs that the realities, challenges and opportunities presented by the Future of Work are being recognized and positively embraced. Perhaps the shift to the new, enlightened 21st century employment deal is already well on the way.

Case in Point 5.2: Buurtzorg

Background

In 2006, Buurtzorg started something of a revolution in healthcare in Netherlands and also illustrated what progressive ways of working and purpose-driven employment arrangements can look like in reality. Initially set up to reduce bureaucracy, increase the quality of healthcare and decrease healthcare costs, Buurtzorg grew to 10,000+ employees with an 8.7 staff satisfaction rate and is present in 25+ countries.

Key Take-aways

o Buurtzorg works on self-managed teams of nurses/healthcare professionals who in turn work on an "onion model" to deliver patient care.

o The heart of the onion model is the person who needs help; the second layer is their informal support network such as family, friends, etc.; the third layer is the Buurtzorg team who are deployed to neighborhoods to holistically understand a patient's needs and to make connections with the fourth layer: healthcare providers in the area.

o This model allows clients to have control over their lives for as long as they are able to and at the same time allows nurses to do their work with professional freedom, ownership, and purpose.

o Self-managed teams are free to organize their own care delivery arrangements and schedules and to host activities and boost morale among their community as they see fit. They also determine many of their own people management processes.

o Buurtzorg's technology support for teams serves to reduce bureaucracy even further.

o With agility and responsiveness to evolving client needs at the heart of what it does, Buurtzorg services have grown to include integrated community care, mental health services, support to young children and their families, and domestic care services using the same model.

Sources

https://www.youtube.com/watch?v=SSoWtXvqsgg&t=69s.
https://www.buurtzorg.com/about-us/.

Where do we go from here?

As we have explored, the talent landscape and the employment deal is changing and changing fast. A more mature understanding between employer and employee will help to trigger new arrangements and support individuals to successfully navigate the Future of Work, while giving employers flexible access to the skills they need to prosper.

This reality, combined with ever-changing ways of getting work done and accessing and managing talent, will fundamentally change how both employers and employees will manage and navigate the employment environment into the future. The employers who win in the changing landscape will be those who are open and honest about the New Deal and who provide the purpose-driven, learning environment, and employee experience that authentically delivers on it. This level of authenticity, and how we deal with our choices around ethical employment practices, requires a new Future of Work leadership perspective and mindset, which is the focus of the next chapter.

What you can do
On the individual level:

- What are you doing to manage your own personal development and career trajectory to remain career-agile into the future?

- How open are you to learning new technology to be more versatile and/or relevant in the future?

- Does the purpose of the organization(s) you work for connect with your own?

- Does the organization you work for provide you with the learning and growth environment you need to secure your own career "future-fitness"?

Case in Point 5.3: Viisi

Background

Viisi is a mortgage advice company based in the Netherlands. Viisi has a clear purpose: let's change finance. The company works with a "people first" principle: employees always come first, followed by clients, and shareholders come last. Since 2010, the company has grown to 60 employees, issued 10,000 mortgages amounting to €3.5B and has a customer satisfaction rate of 9.8 out of 10.

Key Take-aways

o Viisionairs are expected to treat others like they'd like to be treated themselves (the so-called "golden rule").

o Tweaking the Holacracy model of team-based self-organization to suit its needs, Viisi's organizational structure is decentralized and based on circles. The outer circle defines the company's purpose and includes self-governing smaller circles whose goals align with the larger circle they are a part of. Employees can be a part of as many or as few circles as they see fit.

o All circles include a Lead Link (responsible for dividing the roles and priority setting in the circle) and a Rep Link (represents their circle to other circles). The roles are chosen in the circle itself and rotate on a "first among equals" ("*primus inter pares*") basis. This results in decentralized decision-making and knowledge-sharing.

o Pay is but one of the people processes that are run in a very different way at Viisi. Salaries and performance are split. Every Viisionair gets a fixed salary with an annual pay rise. Salaries are transparent and set at the top quartile of the external salary benchmark. The teams check these benchmarks now and then – mainly when new colleagues are hired. If salaries have risen, then salaries of the whole team are adjusted. Performance is a peer-to-peer responsibility and solved in the daily or weekly meetings.

o Individual bonuses were abolished as they undermine cooperation within the team. Fixed salaries create the "psychological safety" to give and receive honest feedback without the concern of negative financial repercussions.

Sources
https://www.youtube.com/watch?v=08iuH7XsdsY
https://leadermorphosis.co/ep-28-tom-van-der-lubbe-on-salaries-and-culture-in-self-managing-organisations
https://corporate-rebels.com/viisi/
https://corporate-rebels.com/less-is-more-10-practical-examples/
https://www.viisi-expats.nl/about-viisi/

On the organizational level:

- How would you describe your "employment deal" today? What could it look like in the future to reflect the Future of Work realities at play for both the organization and for the workforce?

- How prepared are you to deal with change and volatility in terms of your talent and workforce requirements?

- What learning and growth opportunities do you provide in your workplace to ensure your talent continues to match the changing needs of the organization?

- What steps are you taking to create an environment that celebrates authentic and honest communication around the organization's immediate and future needs?

Chapter 6
FUTURE READY LEADERS

What got you here, won't get you there.
Marshall Goldsmith

It is not easy to be a leader today. In the age of a continuously shifting business and talent landscape, leaders are faced with rising expectations from all fronts: boards, executives and shareholders, as well as staff, business partners and customers. On top of increasing demands to run and grow the current business, leaders are expected to transform and adapt their organizations in the face of new technologies, ongoing business disruption and rapidly changing markets and talent requirements– not to mention dealing with the odd global pandemic. It is clear that the changing world of work demands a fresh look at how we lead.

But surely, a leader's role has always required an ability to deal with what is needed in the prevailing landscape of the day, as well as to sense and respond appropriately to emerging and future challenges ahead? It just seems, however, that they must now do this at a pace and against a background of continuous change and uncertainty that sets today's leadership challenges apart from previous generations.

Leadership development trends, models and advice for the new age are in plentiful supply – from digital leadership, to agile leadership, transformational leadership, servant leadership, authentic leadership – the list of remedies and solutions in the ever-growing leadership development industry goes on. Rather than adding to that supply, the aim of this chapter is simply to present and surface some of this evidence and thinking in order for you to shape *your own* personal approach and "model" for leadership in the changing world of work.

Much has been written about the attributes and qualities required to shape and lead the organization of the future. Commonly-quoted essentials of modern leadership – such as embracing new technology, dealing with continuous change, and managing diversity – are currently accepted as "business as usual" rather than anything new.

Writers and commentators, like the global thought leader and bestselling author Peter Fisk, suggest that today's digital leaders need to:

> *... adjust their mindsets to reflect the characteristics of the new business environment: fast-paced, connected, non-linear, virtual and technology-enabled.*

Michael Lurie, a partner at McKinsey, suggests that:

> *The digital economy requires a new kind of leader, one who can energize, build and lead people in a direction that will benefit a complex set of customers and stakeholders.*

Others argue that, despite today's conditions, the fundamental essence of leadership has not changed all that much. Some of the enduring traits of effective leadership from the past remain key to the future. Basic and long-serving qualities like trust, clarity of purpose, relationship building, as well as calm, focused, and shrewd management of capital and resources, remain important guiding principles as they have always been.

But, if this era is so different, then what specific realities and challenges should today's leaders consider for shaping the Future of Work? What is different today compared to a generation or two ago? And, most importantly, what can leaders do in practical terms to adjust and thrive in this new environment?

When it comes to leadership, context is everything. Early adopters in leading increasingly complex and fast-moving environments point to the need for organizations to be more strategically responsive and adaptable, more organizationally agile and also more comfortable in dealing with constant change. Indeed, in these uncertain times, leadership agility is becoming a necessity rather than some episodic or heroic trait only called upon at times of significant challenge or opportunity for the organization. Leadership agility allows those at the helm to continuously and purposefully focus on what is needed in the present, while also being able to respond effectively to the uncertainty and ambiguity of the modern marketplace.

While the focus of this chapter is on the role of a leader, it is increasingly important for *every* individual, regardless of their position, title, or rank to practice leadership as we embrace the Future of Work. And critically, an orientation towards self-leadership was a key competency identified in our research on the necessary skills of the future explored in **Chapter 4.**

Whether you are a leader of a large organization and a leader of leaders, a section manager, an individual contributor, an independent contractor, or a parent, you practice leadership every day simply through the influence of others towards a specific goal – the last few words probably being the simplest definition of leadership out there. It comes down to a matter of perspective on our own individual sphere of influence or locus of control, that determines the specific stage on which our own individual leadership operates and shows up.

> **Leaders cannot lead their organizations if they cannot first lead themselves.**

As we explore the leader's role in the Future of Work a bit further, I hope the principles and ideas discussed here will assist anyone who wants to be more conscious and self-aware about how they practice their leadership, not just in the conduct or the context of a formal or appointed role. In the following pages, we will look at what current practice and research is telling us about:

- The emerging role and functions of the Future of Work leader;
- Relevant leadership models, and how to find your own leadership model and brand;
- Practical features of Future of Work and agile leadership;
- The four habits of the agile or Future of Work leader.

The emerging role of the Future of Work leader

In the WorkMatters research on agility and Future of Work readiness, the business leaders we spoke to agreed that organizations need to be ready to respond to risk and to capitalize on the opportunities that can arise from an increasing variety of sources. They also need to be able to take advantage of the fundamental changes in how work can now be delivered and organized.

The leaders also said that what feels different about their role into the future as compared to the past boils down a combination of four basic leadership functions:

1. **Framing strategy:** The need to focus, as appropriate, on short-term priorities while being open and responsive to what is emerging in the market and the wider environment.

2. **Navigating complexity:** Leading the organization through increased pace of change, complexity, ambiguity, choices, and options.

3. **Shaping culture:** Creating a safe and engaged environment for personal and organizational growth, collaboration, and agility.

4. **Enabling continuous change:** Creating ways of working and a culture where continuous change is enabled and role modeled rather than just a process that needs to be periodically designed and implemented.

These four functions of what agile or Future of Work leader requires create a useful guide for reminding leaders of the key pillars of their daily role in shaping the Future of Work. While the leaders acknowledged that these functions have always existed to some degree or another in the past, the nature of how they are executed in the context for leading the future is changing.

It was notable that enablers, such as digital leadership or entrepreneurial orientation, did not arise in the question of their "core" leadership challenge or role. These were taken as "given" in modern-day leadership, including the openness to have these attributes as part of their own skillset. The leaders also recognized the need for having the right people around them to provide those qualities if they did not naturally possess these qualities themselves.

Framing strategy

When it comes to framing strategy, Rita McGrath captures the need for a more dynamic approach in *The End of Competitive Advantage*, through a combination of:

1. Continuous re-configuration (in response to what is changing around us).
2. Healthy disengagement (with what might have been successful for us in the past).
3. Optimizing resource allocation (to promote deftness and speed).
4. Building innovation proficiency (as a habit).
5. Leadership and mindset.

This strategy highlights the importance of leaders being able to communicate the overall direction and purpose of the organization, or a specific program of work, because the route to that goal and purpose (the what and the how, if you like) will frequently change and get disrupted.

Simon Sinek refers to this in his "Golden Circle" model – and the primacy of the "Why" an organization exists in inspiring purpose-driven action and commitment from the inside out rather than from the outside in.

McKinsey's "Three Horizon" concept (**Figure 6.1**) is also a helpful illustration of the ambidextrous skill of leading for the short and longer terms – at the same time. Horizon 1 emphasizes execution of a company's existing business model, priorities, and core capabilities in the short-term. Horizon 2 extends that outlook to the development of new customers, markets, or targets usually within the existing business model. Horizon 3 is the creation of new capabilities and new business to take advantage of or respond to disruptive opportunities, perhaps peripheral to the organization's current business model and scope.

Our 20th century management models, combined with the short-term demands and expectations of various stakeholders have perhaps conditioned us to focus primarily on Horizons 1 and 2. With some exceptions, we rarely acknowledged the need for deliberate Horizon 3 planning and mostly reacted to trends and events as they evolved.

Figure 6.1: McKinsey's Three Horizon Model

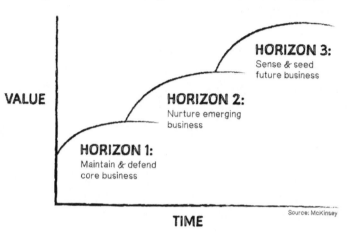

HORIZON 3:
Sense & seed
future business

VALUE

HORIZON 2:
Nurture emerging
business

HORIZON 1:
Maintain & defend
core business

Source: McKinsey

TIME

The shift we see now is from a general recognition of Horizon 3 towards a full-scale and genuine investment in it. Our ongoing attention needs to be on the future of business with a heightened awareness of what is happening around us – and a willingness to challenge the assumptions that underpin Horizon 1 and 2 thinking.

In the past, the lack of attention on Horizon 3 caused many successful organizations to stumble – and stumble badly. Consider Kodak, Nokia, and Sony (among others). It wasn't that these companies and their management were unaware of emerging developments or threats within their industries. But a significant contribution to their future problems arose when deeply-rooted assumptions on the current business model's invincibility and on consumer loyalty to traditionally strong products and services were not sufficiently challenged or tested. Successful execution of Horizons 1 and 2 does not mean the company is bullet-proof for the future, as evidenced by the many giants that have tumbled over the years.

Horizon 3-focused enterprises (such as Apple, Uber, and Airbnb) noted the emerging "sharing economy," accessibility, and relentless connectivity as future realities. Those enterprises used such periphery developments and trends to blow apart the traditional assumptions, expectations, and projections of the narrower lens of Horizon 1 and 2 thinking. The success of longer established organizations, such as Google, Microsoft, and Amazon has (so far), in large part, come down to their ability to incorporate Horizon 3 thinking, experimentation, and application into their existing business models. This strategic mindset opens up a leader's view as to how enabled and Agile the organization needs to be at a wider and more operational level.

Today, these three horizons need to be active at the same time, which is even more reason why leaders need agility and the right diversity of talent around them. They also need to help people focus on the "why" of what the organization is about so that everyone is open to new possibilities and realities.

Navigating complexity

At the core of Future of Work leadership is the willingness to be open to what is happening beyond our strategic limits, to challenge our own assumptions about the continuance of past successes, and a genuine investment into Horizon 3 possibilities. Leadership in these times also presents a complexity challenge. Despite our best efforts and intentions, we are also subject to external events and competition, rapidly developing technology, and changing customer sentiment.

Applying complexity theory to this combination of realities suggests that previously reliable, linear, plan-and-control approaches to organizational leadership need to give way to, or at least combine with, more agile "sense-and-respond" approaches to the new conditions. In navigating complexity, the agile leader's role is to bring as much clarity, reassurance, and simplicity to complex situations, to help people see the wood from the trees, to break problems down, and to prioritize based on the desired outcomes and purpose of a given situation.

Figure 6.2: The Cynefin Model

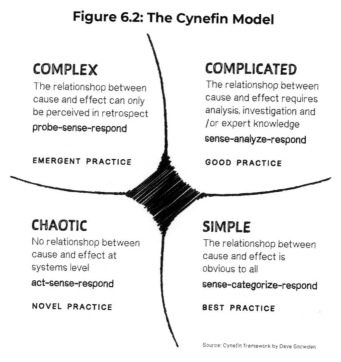

COMPLEX
The relationshop between cause and effect can only be perceived in retrospect
probe-sense-respond

EMERGENT PRACTICE

COMPLICATED
The relationshop between cause and effect requires analysis, investigation and /or expert knowledge
sense-analyze-respond

GOOD PRACTICE

CHAOTIC
No relationshop between cause and effect at systems level
act-sense-respond

NOVEL PRACTICE

SIMPLE
The relationshop between cause and effect is obvious to all
sense-categorize-respond

BEST PRACTICE

Source: Cynefin framework by Dave Snowden

A useful model is Dave Snowden's Cynefin model (**Figure 6.2**), a sense making model which summarizes the increase in complexity we see today – the contrast between what is simple or obvious, what is complicated but logical, and what is genuinely complex. Today's environment requires a heightened capacity to explore emergent solutions. More complex situations require more experimentation, probing, and sensing to try different scenarios. Complex and complicated chunks of work must be broken down to be more obvious and more easily handled. All this requires a leadership style that is comfortable with a complex reality by creating a psychologically safe environment where such emergent and experimental practice can be explored and embraced.

The inescapable truth of leading in a complex environment is that leaders need to have an agile and open mindset to recognize obvious, complicated, or complex scenarios and to lead others accordingly and appropriately. In doing so, they are shaping and nurturing the culture required for sustainable organizational agility.

Shaping culture

Many would argue that culture is probably the most important topic to consider when working on organizational agility. You can have all the strategies, technology, practices, and processes you like but, if the culture in your organization is not open to working in an agile way, then any good intentions for agility will fail.

With so much ambiguity and complexity to navigate, it is futile to think leaders can map out a detailed and linear roadmap for success. We don't hear too much about five-year strategies anymore, clearly signposted with definitive milestones and predictable measurements. Such are the relics of the plan-and-control world, when pace and complexity were more manageable and predictable. No sooner is the ink dry on such a plan than the assumptions underpinning such clarity are disrupted and changed by any number of external or internal factors.

Such definitive paths has been replaced by the necessity to openly and calmly lead in an environment that can and will change ever more frequently than before. Leaders must bring passion and purpose to the direction the organization needs to go, serve those they lead by providing them with what they need to grow, and then to get out of their way! In other words, they set the direction and tone for the organization, create the ecosystem and, most importantly, the culture for success.

Culture is often described as simply the execution mechanism for delivering on the organization's strategy. It determines day-today behavior, collective habits, decision-making, and what gets recognized and rewarded (see **Figure 6.3**). Authors Ricky Moorhead and Gregory Griffin suggested a more elaborate definition of culture as:

> *The set of shared values, often taken for granted, that help people in an organization understand what actions are considered acceptable and which are considered unacceptable. Often communicated through stories or symbols.*

Figure 6.3: Culture: The Mechanism for Executing Strategy

The leader's role of being responsible for the prevailing culture is quite clear, and they need to be deliberate about what their organization aspires to be. Gareth Jones, author of *Who Would Want to Be Led by You?*, summarized it like this: there are essentially two vehicles for converting organizational strategy into results – structure and culture. Leaders need to understand and align both in order to achieve what the organization is there to do.

Edgar Schein, considered the grandfather of culture, captures the relationship between leaders and culture bluntly and well:

The only thing of real importance that leaders do is to create and manage culture. If you do not manage culture, it manages you.

In shaping culture, leaders must be acutely aware of the values and key behaviors that are important to the organization and that enable agile ways of working; behaviors such as collaboration, continuous feedback, encouraging diversity, self-organization, and transparency. Role modeling and consistently reminding people of these agile behaviors and ways of working will make it normal and psychologically safe to act in ways that help them to execute agility more confidently on a day-to-day basis.

Enabling change

Enabling change is the fourth key role of the agile leader, which means helping people to deal with continuous and ongoing change as well as more significant periods of change when they occur. The classic Kubler Ross Change Curve (**Figure 6.4**) highlights the emotional journey people go through during the change process. Awareness of the emotional component helps the agile leader understand the different leadership styles necessary to effectively connect with and guide people through the various natural phases of change. It also provides them with the resources to successfully manage that change.

Adjustment in a leader's energy and approach is required through the three main stages of the change process, reflecting the needs and likely experiences of their team as they go through that change. Early on, it is about informing, explaining and storytelling about the future vision, engaging people by displaying confidence about the change and what is in it of personal benefit and growth for them as individuals as well as for the organization. It is then about energetically and enabling achievement of the "messy middle" of the change, walking the talk, being visible and present with them with understanding and empathy in the messiness and frustration involved in the important middle phase of any change process. And then it is about consolidating that change, equipping them, role modelling new skills, showing trust and recognition in people as they experiment new ways of working in the new state, providing them with the necessary tools and removing obstacles to success. Just simply being aware of the change process (whether big change or small) and the needs of others through the change process will help leaders and those that they lead on a more sustainable basis.

Figure 6.4: The Kubler Ross Change Curve

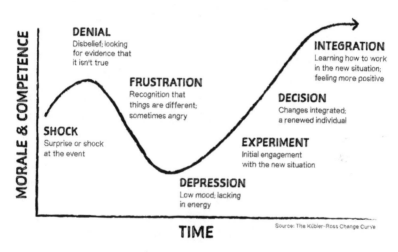

So, at the end of any given day, when you reflect on your role as an agile leader, ask yourself:

- How well did I frame the work and explain the "why" behind what we are doing?
- Are people energized towards that purpose?
- Did I help to simplify and clarify complex issues?

- Did I role model and encourage the right behaviors for agility to thrive?
- Did I provide what was needed to enable change?

Keeping these four key roles of agile leadership top of mind will help prioritize what needs to be done, give people what they need to perform, and provide clarity on what people can do to grow and to contribute.

I recall during the research for this book, James O'Connor, Managing Director and VP of Microsoft International Operations, explaining his three main priorities as a leader at Microsoft of multiple international teams that are multi-disciplinary and geographically complex. His three rules for himself are *"to provide clarity, to create energy and purpose for what we are doing, and to enable success so that colleagues can do their best work."* Simplifying the multi-faceted task of leadership into a few personal habits or leadership principles felt to me a very empowering and liberating practice James had developed to ensure he was keeping on the right track and doing the right things in the midst of a fast paced, continuously and complex environment.

Evolving leadership models

There are so many models around leadership today and no shortage of well-meaning advice and experience. In searching for our own leadership model and practice, it is worth considering a few relevant and established models of leadership, if only to help to frame and label your own personal practices and approach.

Leadership development experts and commentators have identified and been vocal about the shift from traditional "command-and-control" leadership styles to more transformational, agile leadership approaches over the last several decades. In *Leadership Agility*, William Joiner and Stephen

Joseph define the natural and progressive development stages of the agile leader, as detailed in **Figure 6.5**.

Figure 6.5: Features of Agile Leadership

AGILE LEADERSHIP LEVEL	KEY FEATURES
1: EXPERT	o Subject matter/domain expertise, positional authority o Success through incremental improvements to existing strategy o Largely tactical, task-focused, supervisory
2: ACHIEVER	o Motivated to achieve outcomes important to the organization o Motivating others recognized as important/strategic o Successful where episodic shifts in strategy and change exist o Strategic, outcomes-oriented, managerial
3: CATALYST	o Facilitative, visionary, sees beyond current organizational strategy and sets out to create a participative culture o Longer-term, open, growth and change-oriented, communicates the "why" and not just the "what, how and when" o Successful in a high change, volatile environment

Source: Joiner & Joseph.

As this figure suggests, the Level 1 leader evokes the traditional, short-term focused, tactical and problem-solving orientation of the Expert Leader. Level 2 represents the broader focused, strategic and outcome-oriented Achiever Leader, and Level 3 presents the more visionary and facilitative/empowering Catalyst Leader. These levels were researched and identified through the lens of managing in complex and agile work environments. While all three levels resonate and are needed in different scenarios, the relevance and appropriateness of the Catalyst Leader attributes have been more evident in recent times to lead through increasingly complex and rapidly changing work environments. Again, the agile Leader knows when to apply these levels or styles – and why.

A Servant Leadership mindset unlocks the conditions for agility.

Many leaders advocate for the facilitative and growth-oriented approach of what is called Servant Leadership. This approach provides a helpful and relevant default stance to modern-day leadership and the principles of leadership we have been discussing in this chapter. Essentially, the concept indicates a leader who views his or her role as one of support to those they lead, rather a position of authority and personal power.

A Servant Leadership mindset unlocks the conditions for agility through qualities like empowerment, trust, and openness. Servant leadership, therefore, is a naturally forward-looking and growth-oriented position. It triggers much greater outcomes in terms of engagement and commitment than the traditional, command-and-control ideas of the mid-20th century. Servant leadership builds on the contrasting leadership styles of Douglas McGregor's Theory X (people need supervision and rules to function) *versus* Theory Y (people are inherently motivated to do good work and should be inspired to do so).

An interesting take on this growth-oriented leadership positioning is Steve Radcliffe's FED (Future, Engage, Deliver) Model. Like the servant leader concept, it is based on providing a future oriented context to every leadership action and behavior. If the leader, and more importantly the follower, focuses on what they are doing to make things better for the future – and their future in particular – they are able to establish a mindset and an openness to more positive conversations, engagement, outcomes, and innovation.

Finding your own leadership brand

The models highlighted above are just a few examples for the purpose of providing guidance, insight, and perhaps a label and idea or two for you to consider for your own unique and personal stance and leadership practice. Essentially, it is about thinking through your own preferred brand and running with it in a deliberate and mindful way. Being yourself with skill will allow you to bring the best of yourself to your role and to those you lead.

In leading the organization of the future, there is a temptation to think there is some perfect leadership style or persona out there. Perhaps all you need to do is somehow change your DNA to fit a specific, perfect model? The best Future of Work leaders we have encountered don't go there... trying to copy someone else's style or a textbook model is ultimately unsustainable. People will eventually see through it, which only adds to your complications. Each of us already has a leadership brand, whether we are aware of it or not. The questions are:

- How aware we are of it?
- What do we want to do with it?

The effective leaders I've researched and worked with have a clear picture of the leadership style or brand that is comfortable for them. They learn from approaches that speak to them and from their own role models, honing their habits and skills around that "brand." They are aware of their blind spots and develop strategies to compensate for them, either through coaching, or by simply surrounding themselves with diverse colleagues who are strong in the areas they are weak.

In the WorkMatters research, a number of features specifically related to agile leadership in the Future of Work consistently emerged which might also help as a checklist of sorts for your own leadership approach:

1. Mindset.
2. Self-awareness.
3. Build your best team.
4. Show people the way and let them get on with it.
5. Identify your own "best boss" habits.
6. Show appreciation and provide feedback.

1. Mindset

Marshall Goldsmith, author of *What Got You Here, Won't Get You There* (and the quote at the start of this chapter), claims that leadership agility is the most important competency for leaders today. Goldsmith is clear in proposing agility as a competency, not a model. The importance of an agile mindset, from the individual perspective, was discussed at length in **Chapter 3**. Leaders are, first and foremost, individuals and as such, need to adopt the agile mindset, for which self-awareness is the cornerstone.

2. Self-awareness

Awareness of your own leadership strengths and skills, blind spots, and emotional triggers is essential in the modern work environment. It is much easier to manage stressful situations when you're acting in a deliberate, self-aware manner. So, becoming more cognizant of your own leadership brand and mental model is necessary for being yourself. Self-awareness and humility regarding our own behavior is helpful for leading any organization, and especially so for a leader seeking to create a working culture associated with organizational agility.

3. Build your best team

Armed with clarity around the Future of Work leader's role, an agile mindset, and self-awareness, leaders also need to look at who they hire, promote, and keep within their future organization. No leader can succeed alone in an increasingly complex environment. Having the right talent at all levels is critical as organizations evolve and grow.

There is an increasing need for diversity of skills and knowledge on leadership teams, plus a keen awareness around the many different ways of getting work done, and sources to locate talent. Building your best team may include resetting your expectations and relationship with your HR colleagues, who are tapped into the current talent landscape, accustomed to the working realities of the new employment deal, and who are in an important position to support you in shaping the Future of Work.

4. Show the way and let them get on with it

The adaptive and agile leader sets clear ground rules and parameters, clarifies and explains the purpose and direction the organization is headed, and then lets their teams get on with it. In a supportive environment of trust and clear goals, employees will respond and thrive under such conditions.

Leaders need to develop other leaders and employees around them who will seek and accept autonomy and accountability, because no one has the time to be everywhere and on everyone's case. With some space and process guidance provided for regular review and open feedback, the team can course-correct itself and hold each other to account, without you in the room. An agile team-working culture significantly reduces the time you will need to spend on supervision, which allows you to focus on other things.

We are in the age of the authentic leader, which should help to end the pretense and pressure of achieving perfection, benefiting leaders themselves and those whom they lead. Leaders cannot be expected to have all the answers for everyone who demands them. Showing vulnerability is an essential building block of trust and invites others to share the load. Employees will respect rather than doubt you. Most importantly, they will follow your example, creating a safe environment where problems – as well as innovations and opportunities – will be aired freely without the fear of ridicule or blame. Creating a psychologically safe environment is probably one of the most important leadership contributions you will ever make. Change will be embraced rather than avoided.

5. Identify your own "best boss" habits

While searching for your authentic self and the ingredients of your own leadership brand, think about what author and consultant Chris Roebuck refers to as the simple and impactful behaviors and habits that made your "best boss" memorable and motivating to you.

> **Leadership agility is probably the most important competency for leaders today.**

What would your team say to the same question about you?

Identify these trademark habits that come naturally to you and use them often.

Encourage other leaders working for you to do the same, and develop leaders who can help you deliver on your goals and create the working culture you want to see.

6. Show appreciation and provide feedback

To reinforce an agile, accountable, and trusting working culture, feedback is essential. Don't allow problems to fester and develop. Celebrate success. Shift the balance to behaviors you want to see.

People will soon figure out the right way of doing things under your watch. Generate a climate of enablement and empowerment, rather than control and compliance. This shift alone will unleash talent, performance and engagement in your teams.

Creating a habit of appreciative feedback and demonstrating to people that you have their back will then allow you to have the tough conversations when needed. Such conversations may still sting a little but they will be more readily accepted and trusted. People will know the feedback is given with the intention of enabling positive growth and not correcting fault.

The 4 Cs of Agile Leadership

These Future of Work leadership habits, combined with what we know from our own experiences of the enduring qualities that go into being a good boss, will help leaders thrive in the new landscape and allow others to do the same. There are many examples of this empowered leadership style out there. Which leadership brands speak to you?

Figure 6.6: The 4 Cs of Agile Leadership

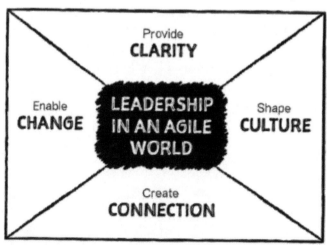

Figure 6.6 summarizes much of what we have explored in terms of agile leadership in this chapter and reminds us of the regular habits and behaviors that will keep us on a path towards agile leadership while so much else is going on around us.

The 4 Cs or *habits* of agile leadership are:

1. **The habit of providing clarity to those around us:** Helping others to navigating complexity, reminding and energizing them about the "why" and purpose of what they are doing, framing and sense-making of what is going on and breaking complex situations down to the complicated or obvious.

2. **The habit of shaping culture:** Reinforcing and role modelling the way we do things around here, demonstrating and promoting agile values and behaviors that we talked about such as collaboration, trust and transparency.

3. **Enabling change:** Demonstrating servant leadership, remembering change is about changing hearts as well as minds, showing empathy, providing the necessary resources and support for people to do their work and make change happen.

4. **Creating connection:** Foundational to the other three, creating connection is about building relationships and trust, connecting at both the emotional as well as the rational level. Known social practices such as empathy, humility, gratitude and positive enquiry provide a culture of trust, empowerment and ultimately agility.

Case in Point 6.1: Microsoft

Background

By 2014, Microsoft faced a number of external and internal challenges in the midst of shifting consumer demands and global competition. A culture shift was needed to move the organization from an era of extreme competitiveness and historically successful business models and behaviors to a more open and learning culture that could adapt to rapid change in all its core sectors. New CEO, Satya Nadella, was instrumental in changing the culture at the top from a "know it all" to a "learn it all" culture and ways of working.

Key Takeaways

o Senior Management Team training was increased on areas such as growth mindset and empathy, and every SMT weekly meeting started with "Research of the Amazing", spotlighting innovation within Microsoft, which in turn encouraged workplace harmony.

o Failures were encouraged as part of the process and were dealt with empathetically rather than being called out as career-limiting mistakes. The culture was built around a more generous and open learning and growth approach.

o Internal company messaging changed on signage, elevator doors, cups, and so on to reflect a clear message of diversity, inclusion, and empathy.

o Annual organization-wide hackathons were instituted to encourage innovation, empowerment, engagement, ownership, and team building.

o Microsoft's strategy post-2014 changed from hastily releasing stand-alone products to more inclusive products that worked well with competitor ecosystems.

o Change in company culture has had a significant impact on the company's bottom line. Between 2014 and 2020 Microsoft's valuation grew from $300 billion to almost $2trillion.

Sources

PRESENTING: Satya Nadella employed a "growth mindset" to overhaul Microsoft's cutthroat culture and turn it into a trillion-dollar company — here's how he did it
https://www.businessinsider.com/microsoft-ceo-satya-nadella-company-culture-shift-growth-mindset-2020-3?r=US&IR=T.
Transforming Culture at Microsoft: Satya Nadella Sets a New Tone:
https://www.intheblack.com/articles/2018/06/01/satya-nadella-transforming-culture-microsoft.

Where do we go from here?

We don't have all the details about what our organizations will look like tomorrow. The dramatic changes we have already experienced in the first quarter of the 21st century have provided enough evidence for the need to be able to adapt to other disruptions and surprises that surely lie ahead. Nonetheless, the roles and habits of an open and agile leadership approach, a deliberate and authentic leadership brand, and a keen eye for talent and diversity will help leaders navigate whatever emerges in the future.

Overall, leaders will need to:

- Have the strategic and sensory capability to identify the business and operational models appropriate for a changing future;
- Understand the options around mobilizing different forms of labor, talent, and enabling technology;
- Create high performing work cultures that keep the organization agile and learning so that it can both execute efficiently today and adapt for what is needed tomorrow.

Knowing more about the qualities of a Future of Work leader, we can set about designing a talent management strategy that puts the right leaders and people in place to deal with the inevitable changes as they continue to emerge and develop.

Developing a Future of Work leadership mindset that considers a clear purpose about who we are as individuals and as an organization, and what we are trying to achieve – is a surely critical first step. Having this purposeful, but open and honest perspective will help to create the space for developing a more authentic, comfortable and personal style of leadership for the future.

Case in Point 6.2: Roche

Background

Roche, a biotechnology firm, was looking for ways of working that would ensure long-term success in a constantly changing competitive environment. The company was also focused on ways in which it could be ready to respond to any situation at any given time. Adopting an agile mindset through agile ways of working was the chosen solution, driven by the leadership team and the recognition that agile thinking and behavior needs to start from the top.

Key Takeaways

o Kinesis was a four-day program, created for 1,000 leaders across the organization.

o Day one included a 360-degree assessment that showed leadership how their behaviors and mindsets directly impacted effectiveness. It forced attendees to confront limiting patterns that might have worked in the past but may not in the future.

o Day 2 was a workshop on the agile mindset and agile ways of working.

o Day 3 got management to re-imagine the organization with more agile processes, structures, and work culture.

o Day 4 included a real-life experiment, where attendees got to implement their ideas and structure during the day with more agility.

o Leadership was then *invited* to use the tools they'd learned, not told to do so. 95% of attendees ran follow-up sessions with their teams and eventually switched over the agile ways of working.

Sources

https://www.mckinsey.com/business-functions/organization/our-insights/how-a-healthcare-company-is-pursuing-agile-transformation.

https://www.mckinsey.com/business-functions/organization/our-insights/doing-vs-being-practical-lessons-on-building-an-agile-culture.

> **We are in the age of the authentic leader – ending the pretense and pressure of achieving perfection.**

A critical partner in sharing the leader's responsibility for shaping the Future of Work is the HR Leader, and those that have a role in shaping people and processes, employee experience, and culture in your organization. This is why we explore the HR leadership role in the next chapter.

What you can do

On the individual level:

- What is your own leadership model and your signature habits? How would you characterize your leadership style and what model do you follow to address changing employee needs and requirements?
- Who was your best boss and why?
- What habits could you develop to fulfil the 4 Cs of the Agile Leader?

On the organizational level:

- Is your leadership development program (or programs) capturing the mindset and skillset required of the agile and future-fit leader?
- Do your management and leadership succession and promotion processes reflect the skills and attributes required to be a future-fit leader?
- What small opportunities and change projects could you identify that would help build agile leadership skills, capability and experience through the organization.

Chapter 7
FUTURE READY HR

The best way to predict the future is to create it.
Abraham Lincoln

While leaders, managers and fellow colleagues ultimately dictate the day-to-day experience of employees, the HR function plays a key role in influencing and often controlling many of the key organizational levers that create and enable that experience. More than any other organizational function or department, HR determines how people strategy, culture, leadership, and the organization of work fuse together (or don't). Whether the topic is workforce planning, recruitment, rewards, training, employee experience, or countless other employee "touch points," HR's hand and influence is there to see. As we will find in this chapter, this influence has grown over the years and there is a new wave of contribution and influence to come. While the term and label of "HR" is well on the way out due to its old-fashioned insinuation of humans as expendable resources to be optimized like other assets and materials in an organization, we use the term here as familiar shorthand to describe the people profession and those who lead that work.

Despite this role and influence on the employee experience, when it comes to public relations, HR can get a tough old time. I recall one HR leader telling me that the role sometimes feels like being a parent to teenagers. Trying to do the right thing but often perceived as getting in the way; accused of not quite being "with it;" attentively and continuously tending to others' needs but seldom satisfying them; seen as out of step and interfering; and constantly getting it in the neck for their trouble! But, at the same time, HR fulfills an invaluable and necessary role and, like that parent, is ultimately, a critical source of support, guidance and care.

Whatever the reputation, brand, or image it has had in the past, HR now has a critical role in shaping the Future of Work. And it will continue to play an increasingly vital role in how our organizations and our workforces are shaped and made ready for the challenges ahead.

In this chapter, we'll reflect on the HR's role, both where it originated and the key challenges it now faces, in shaping the Future of Work. We will also explore what is changing and should change for the function as it charts its new path into the future.

HR then

As you might expect, the evolution of HR has tracked the very evolution of work itself. In understanding the role in the present and future, it is helpful to consider where the profession originated and the functions it has acquired over the decades.

It was not that long ago that HR, or the Personnel Department as it was commonly known, was not exactly regarded as a source for strategic guidance or leadership. Kept firmly in the compliance or "recruitment, pay, and pensions" box, the function has a history of being charged mainly with keeping industrial peace, delivering basic employment services, and generally keeping an organization staffed up and out of trouble on the people front. Such a recount, however, does not accurately reflect how the profession has developed over time and, more importantly, how the role of HR is positioned to influence the world of work to come.

While many fine and authoritative accounts of HR's evolution exist from the likes of Professor Dave Ulrich and others, Dr. Jean Cushen of Maynooth University has an interesting take on the prominent accounts. Following Robert Walton's influential work in the 1980s for the *Harvard Business Review*, she explains the oscillation of HR's role over the decades between phases of "control *versus* commitment" in the world of work. Managerial emphasis has routinely shifted between attempts to tightly prescribe employee efforts and behavior, on the one hand, and fostering a work environment that motivates employees to offer up their best efforts on the other. The following brief trip through the evolution of work (and HR) provides a rough summary of HR's shifting role through the lens of control and commitment.

Industrial Revolution: Control

Arguably, the Industrial Revolution (loosely 1760 to 1840) was the first "modern" example of the formal organization of work, as we know it today. It was triggered by the technological advances of the time, particularly steam power in the late 18th century. The era of artisan cottage industries, and the original "gig workers" gave way to formal organization and work orchestration within factory walls. Employer power and discretion was total and collective. Worker rights did not exist in any formal way. The basic (and necessary) tasks of hiring, paying, and firing workers were all part of the "master's" business day or that of their underlings. This was the ultimate era for employer control, albeit in the absence of formal HR, which was not yet born.

Welfare capitalism: Commitment

The first concerted effort to care for the "human" at work arguably emerged *via* the practice of "welfare capitalism" in the late 1800s.

As industrialization developed in the earlier part of the 19th century, leaders were faced with coordinating and overseeing mass labor for the first time. Planning and supervising work was the priority; the quality of the employees' conditions was not. Over time, relations between employees and supervisors became increasingly confrontational and dysfunctional.

Industrial unrest exposed how employee well-being went hand in hand with productivity. Early pioneers of welfare capitalism, who introduced policies of caring for the welfare of employees and their families, reaped the rewards in the form of hard work and loyalty.

HR is in a position to play a critical role in shaping the Future of Work.

Welfare capitalism was first noted in the US in the late 1800s at the Pullman and Vanderbilt organizations. The practice was often motivated by a sense of moral and religious duty held by leading industrialists concerned with the living conditions and behaviors they observed in the emerging urban centers. However, the productivity gains and industrial peace harnessed by these organizations caused wider uptake of these practices. Through caring for employees and their family's physical, medical, educational and spiritual needs, individuals became bound to the organizations beyond simple wages and it was the first instance of employees identifying with the organization goals.

In the UK, Edward and George Cadbury's "Experiments in Industrial Organization" popularized the core belief of welfare capitalism, namely that:

... the supreme principle is that business efficiency and the welfare of employees are but different sides of the same coin.

The trend also appeared in Ireland where the Guinness family embraced the benefits of welfare capitalism. The stout brewer's medical, housing, and pension arrangements were celebrated to the extent they rendered laboring Guinness men "more eligible for marriage as they could provide for a family dead or alive." Evidence of their building works and amenity provision for workers and the surrounding community is still visible today. These early advocates of welfare capitalism spoke of "improving the conditions and temperament of the workingmen."

The first employee welfare roles emerged in organizations in the form of welfare secretaries – individuals who administrated the benefits and practices targeted at creating a certain type of employee and a certain, basic type of employment experience. The success of welfare capitalism saw a powerful idea take hold, namely that organizations could and should shape and develop people by taking some responsibility for the welfare of workers within their employment. Furthermore, doing so would stimulate one workforce to work harder than another and thus emerged the first instance of the "people advantage."

Scientific management: Control

Throughout the 1900s, organizations grew rapidly due to increasing consumer demand for products or services. Complexity undermined management's ability to plan and regulate workers' behaviors and organizing work became fragmented, chaotic and reactive. Production engineers observed the dysfunction and, irritated by how their new machines were being underused, they began to apply the principles of their discipline to the organization and management of work. This prompted the earliest notions of best practice and the ideal employee, termed the "first class man," whose work methods and output excelled his peers.

With renowned engineering consultant Frederick Taylor leading the way, "Scientific Management" emerged to identify and standardize the most efficient methods of task completion. The efficiency drive ushered in a focus on employees that went beyond welfare and benefits. Instead, the focus shifted to the minutiae of how work was performed. A new range of people-centered practices emerged to support efficiency, including results-based compensation, carefully designed jobs, recruitment benchmarks, and employee and supervisor training

However, the belief that there was one best way to perform work often translated into rigid control of employees, which eventually nurtured an excessively adversarial workplace. Repetitive work and punishment for any deviation from prescribed behavior created industrial unrest, high turnover, and unpredictable work environments. (In some organizations, even smiling was forbidden.)

This was the era that Douglas McGregor would (decades) later describe as Theory X management, which was essentially a preference for the authoritarian, task-based, command-and-control style of managing people. It was the belief that people needed to be commanded in order to perform. In contrast, McGregor also presented Theory Y, which presumed that people wanted to participate in work in a meaningful way and they naturally possessed a growth-oriented approach. Ultimately, under scientific management, the pendulum swung too far away from employee needs and organizations began to pay a price for dismissing the "human" side to their resources.

Human relations: Commitment

The First World War marked another important period for progression in work and work practices. One influence was the huge increase of female participation in the workplace due to so many men being sent to the battlefield and the related surge in industrial output and demand. Workers were recruited *en masse* and expected to manufacture ever more sophisticated products and equipment. The additional complexity and diversity required more involved methods of organizing and delivering work, including more enlightened methods of training, development, and progression.

Other influences came into play around this time, too. Elton Mayo, a Harvard scholar, and an early Taylorite interested in ergonomics, visited the Hawthorne plant in Illinois to evaluate working conditions combining ideas from engineering, psychology, sociology and anthropology. Mayo's famous analysis of the Hawthorne plant in the 1920s and 1930s, known as the "Hawthorne Studies," is credited for uncovering the central role that social relations play within organizations. Mayo and his team followed the behaviors and productivity of teams amidst varying working conditions. A key finding was the influence of team dynamics on work and how first-line supervisors could determine whether a team would advance or obstruct a firm's objectives. In direct opposition to scientific management's control style, Mayo introduced the notion of human relations, which sought appreciation for the idea that employees were social beings at work, driven by a need for belonging and collaboration, just as people are outside of the work setting and environment. Furthermore Mayo and his team, over the course of their studies, asked workers for ideas and realized that, far from needing punitive micro-management, in the right culture people will work harder when given responsibility and autonomy.

Mayo and others, such as Douglas McGregor's pivotal work in the mid-20th century on the human side of enterprise (1960), spawned an appreciation amongst leaders that interpersonal relationships within teams are essential for workplace harmony. They recognized that the team is the center from which behavioral and productive norms emerge. Consequently, a new managerial task emerged – the cultivation of healthy teams through advanced managerial motivational and communication skills.

Mayo sought appreciation for the idea that employees were social beings at work, driven by a need for belonging and collaboration.

Whereas welfare capitalism sought to address industry's problems by socializing employees through building their families and communities around the firm, the human relations movement sought to transform social relations and to professionalize management of people inside the organization. This appreciation for organizational culture and dynamics created additional people responsibilities. HR, in its more modern form, had arrived.

Personnel management: Control

Throughout the 1960s, an appreciation for the complexity of the human side of organizations was widespread. The concepts underpinning organizational psychology, industrial relations, and personnel administration were emerging in business schools as distinct disciplines of expertise. Mid-level managers and corporate executives increasingly participated in leadership training and management development to enhance their self-awareness, communication, and interpersonal skills.

However, leaders' ability to optimize the employment experience was somewhat compromised by the role trade unions played, which collectively negotiated terms and conditions of work. Those terms and conditions could not be adjusted without further collective negotiations and agreements. Although this provided a sense of financial security to employees, it also eroded opportunities for organic individual growth and development and, in doing so, held back the principles of creative job design.

Personnel departments were commonplace and were tasked with administering and upholding collective agreements, while attempting to adhere to the wave of newly-introduced employment legislation and deal with grievances. The personnel department focused on administration of the people side of an organization; the dissemination of trade union approved practices. While the personnel department served to embed concern for people at work into a distinct and essential department, the primary focus was on maintaining industrial peace, not necessarily fostering engagement or competitive advantage through people. The rigidity that the collective agreement model placed on work and careers, and the lack of leadership commitment to a more ambitious engagement approach, constrained the strategic contribution of personnel professionals and the pursuit of the more creative and progressive practices we see today.

Human resource management: Commitment

Throughout the second half of the 20th century and with the arrival of the computer age, the nature of work in developed economies changed as leading organizations shifted from primarily trading products to trading knowledge. Leading authors, notably Peter Drucker, heralded the emergence of the knowledge worker and subsequent essential role of strong cultural approaches to management.

Knowledge work led the way for cultural approaches to people management and an emerging rejection of the adversarial "them versus us" attitude between management and employees. New forms of work and cultural management emerged rapidly, most visibly within high technology and professional services firms.

In these new organizations, the optimum work process, supported by enabling technology, is one that empowers and motivates workers to cultivate and share their valuable knowledge. In practice, this shift saw firms return to the principles of Human Relations and the centrality of corporate culture as a device for managing work. Organizations that wished to design a unique employment experience worked to create a more direct engagement approach with the workforce, either with or without the participation and influence of trade unions. Thus, the practice of Human Resource Management (HRM) fully emerged to signify a departure from, or at least an addition to, the mainly transactional personnel approach. HRM offered a new and distinct proposition, focused on building a relationship between the individual and the firm, not on managing employees *via* external trade unions.

Due to the initial low level of take up, HRM was generally criticized as being "old wine in new bottles." Over time, however, with the development of comprehensive, bundled, cultural approaches to people management, the specialist HR function emerged as a strategically central component to the development of the firm, as noted by writers and researchers such as Ulrich and Dulebohn.

Diffusion of new HR techniques in areas such as selection testing, development, reward, and communications became commonplace. HR departments modeled themselves using the highly influential Ulrich model that highlighted key roles such as the employee champion, administrative expert, change agent, and strategic partner.

Mirroring the rapid change in work and work models we have seen over the second half of the 20th century, HR also has seen an acceleration in its evolution during that time. What began as an administratively-focused personnel model grew into a more strategic function. People, leadership, and culture became recognized as necessary sources of competitive advantage to be intentionally developed.

Indeed, academics and writers such as John McMackin and Margaret Heffernan of Dublin City University described four quite distinct waves of HR evolution since the 1950s, in itself demonstrating the rapidly evolving world of work since that time. In addition to what was going on in HR, many factors contributed to a "war for talent" such as an increasing global talent supply shortage, continued enlightenment into motivation theory, and the individual's pursuit of greater satisfaction and engagement at work. The pressure on HR functions to compete for and retain talent in the workforce intensified, exacerbated by popular work-related theory such as Daniel Pink's identification of Purpose, Autonomy, and Mastery (from his book *Drive*) as critical employee motivators at work. HR was tasked to deliver better work experiences, practices, and benefits to attract and motivate an increasingly expectant workforce.

HR *now*

Since the late 20th century, the HR function has broadened its remit beyond all recognition from its inception, with the need for organizations to recruit, retain, engage, and develop its talent in an increasingly competitive global marketplace. Progressive HR and talent management practices have now spread around the world. With a greater understanding of the business impact of people-oriented drivers, such as culture, employee engagement, and leadership effectiveness, HR found itself with a seat at the executive table. The function is now clearly charged with both its traditional control and compliance-oriented role, as well as a strategic and developmental accountability for an organization's workforce, employee experience, and human capital strategy.

In more recent years, HR has further shifted its emphasis from internal efficiency and effectiveness to external relevance and contribution. Dave Ulrich, referred to by *HR Magazine* as "the

Father of HR" for his leading contribution to advancing the profession over the last 30 years, captured the idea of HR's transition over the decades. He recognizes its transformation from an "inside out" looking function – servicing the needs of the business – to a more "outside in" looking function.

HR's contribution to the world of work

While the function may have its critics (What function operates to its full potential all the time?), it is worth remembering what HR has contributed to the world of work and to wider society. Some examples serve to illustrate this contribution. In the main, it has:

- Provided a critical balance between business delivery and employee well-being and fairness;
- Acted as the first responder in the tougher aspects of corporate life, from minor disruptions and internal disputes to handling the workforce and human consequences of large-scale events such as 9/11, the financial crisis, or the COVID-19 pandemic;
- Helped navigate employees through inevitable business and personal crises in as humane ways as possible;
- Often served as the champion of progressive people policies and a critical player in preserving industrial peace, sometimes at critical junctures in the survival of the business;
- Prevented the worst excesses of corporate and worker exploitation, promoting fairness and equity when, without their presence, employee outcomes could have been worse;
- Served as a major source of support to leaders, managers, and employees when needed most.

At no time was HR's impact more vivid than during the COVID-19 crisis. The department needed to lead from the front in what was, first and foremost, a human crisis in virtually every home and workplace across the globe. Commentary from the likes of the *Harvard Business Review* and *The Economist* compared HR's elevated leadership role in COVID-19 times to the CFO's role during the 2008 financial crisis.

In truth, HR's value as a full and equal member around the C-suite table has been developing for some time. And today, HR's job is firmly about making the organization competitive and successful in the marketplace though effective deployment, leadership, and development of its people.

This progression of the function within the C-suite has also been evidenced by the increasing "inter-changeability" of top executives who are now moving into the HR chair from the business arena and *vice versa*. For example, the Musgrave Group, Ireland's largest food wholesaler and retailer, is led by Chief Executive Noel Keeley who served as HRD in the company and elsewhere for many years. James Ryan, COO of several organizations including Bluebridge Technologies and Ammeon, is an experienced HR Director. Aisling Teillard, co-founder and CEO of Our Tandem, the digital employee experience solutions company, was a senior HR leader with the likes of O2 and SAP. On the other hand, Ger Mitchell, Chief HR Officer (and previously Commercial Director) of Permanent tsb, Ireland's third largest bank, and Loren Shuster, Global Chief People Officer of Lego, both worked as senior commercial executives in their organizations. Such organizations realize that people are not just resources to be utilized and organized in a business; they are the business, and they expect their people leaders to be full and equal contributors at the executive table. Former Commercial Director, Ger Mitchell clearly explains his thinking when taking up his executive HR leadership role:

A CHRO / HRD has to have a genuine and authentic belief in the potential of people, the power of the collective, as well as having a compelling vision for the role of HR as the key strategic enabler within an ever changing business environment. It is simply critical therefore that Commercial and People strategies are infused with and by each other.

The natural progression for the HR leader and the wider HR function is therefore not just implementing blanket solutions, but also sensing future talent needs, and leading change and innovation. Gone are the days of reactively "serving" (sometimes dressed up as "partnering") management's business needs. The essential and compliance-oriented needs and accountabilities of HR are important, but they should not define the perceived value that the function has to offer into the future. Part of HR's challenge will be accepting the new strategic expectation and adopting the capacity, capability, resources, and mindset to match its future mandate and its potential to shape the Future of Work.

> **HR's role as the chief architect of work is an opportunity to take and to shape how, where, and by whom work is done in the future.**

The history of HR's journey simply serves as a reminder of where HR has come from, the legacy it has as a function, and ultimately, what it has been mandated to do by the prevailing leadership agenda of the day. It also serves as a reminder to HR to be mindful of what kind of legacy it wants to create in the new world of work into the future. What will the history books of HR say about the role and contributions of the profession in 2050 or in 2075?

Where next for HR?

Looking to the future, the "outside-in," business leadership role of HR, uniquely mandated with a human focus and championing the employee experience, will be required more than ever as we navigate through the Fourth Industrial Revolution. Whether it is to enable greater strategic agility, implement digital transformation or explore new business models and ways of getting work done though technology or other employment trends, people and workforce strategy will be central to an organization's ultimate success as it responds to continuous change in the marketplace. Further evolution and disruption to the employee experience and agenda are also inevitable, a shifting reality that needs proactive leadership and workplace innovation. Who is better placed to deal with these challenges than a freshly purposed, equipped and mandated HR profession?

This current and future scenario poses great opportunity but also significant challenges for HR. One of the dangers is that the people agenda has become increasingly broad. How can it deliver on the already diverse and expansive expectations of employees and leaders for both "traditional" services and also a broadening remit into the future?

The Future of Work poses four particular challenges to HR, in addition to ongoing talent, workforce, and organizational changes:

1. Shaping the Future of Work.
2. Embracing the new work landscape and employee experience.
3. Adoption and application of emerging technology.
4. Dealing with complexity, uncertainty, and continuous change.

Shaping the Future of Work

As we have explored throughout this book, the Future of Work is an ill-defined and sprawling subject. One aspect of the Future of Work is how we are entering a major re-set phase of how work "gets done." As we have all experienced, huge shifts have already happened in the technology software development area. Traditional ways of working in that sector have become unsustainable due to the pace of change, rapid technological advancement, and increased customer demands. The unsustainability of traditional work practices, skills, processes, and structures started in tech and has since spread to other functions and industries. While traditional work practices and structures won't disappear overnight, the movement towards more agile ways of working to manage rapid change is clear. These factors, combined with changing expectations amongst the current and next generation of employees, creates quite an agenda for the HR team and leaders of the future.

The Future of Work affects all functions within an organization, but the impact on the role of HR is probably the most profound. HR influences so many of the processes and "touch points" that create the overall employee experience, which makes them a critical broker and player for future-fit organizations. How work is designed, how people are recruited, what skills are needed, how leaders are selected and developed, and how a continuous learning culture is delivered are just some of the processes that will be necessary in future-proofing our organizations and our workforces. As Mihaly Nagy, founder and CEO of the HR Summit Congress Series, says:

HR has been offered an unparalleled opportunity to question our biggest paradigms about one of the most fundamental human activities: where people spend most of their awaken time – at work. Work and career as we knew it has changed and changed for good.

But how equipped and resourced is HR for this growing mandate and challenge? And what are the key shifts it needs to make to thrive and take up the challenge of being the architect in chief for the Future of Work and the new Industrial Age?

More than ever before in its history, HR needs to embody the Future of Work mindset for the organizations it serves. In previous business cycles over the last 100 years, HR has been able to adapt, react, and respond to changing organizational needs and talent circumstances. Now, HR's role as the chief architect of work provides an opportunity to *proactively* take and own a starring role in shaping how, where, and by who (or what) work is done into the future. At the very minimum, HR will need to adopt the mindset of what Kevin Mulcahy refers to as a Future of Work "Activist" in his excellent book, *The Future Workplace Experience*. Kevin goes on to suggest that, as well as being a Future of Work Activist itself, HR has a critical role in hiring, encouraging and developing other such Future of Work-minded people and activists throughout all levels and functions of the wider organization.

Embracing the new work landscape and employee experience
Accessing, engaging and utilizing the right skills and talent for a rapidly changing Future of Work requires an HR team with the mindset for embracing that change. New business and organizational models are challenging many of our assumptions regarding work design, talent strategy, and HR management. For example, if an organization is to be re-configured to take advantage of the business and cost benefits of a blended mix of suppliers, outsourcing partners, free agents, automation, and a core, full-time workforce, it follows that a new work design and workforce planning strategy is needed to map out the organization's short and long-term talent needs. A refresh of the employment deal as explored earlier in **Chapter 5** for all worker

categories and not just full time employees is needed to create a broad-based and diverse workforce "community."

Indeed, the management and engagement of the non-core workforce will become a highly strategic function, as consideration must be given to how the different parts of the organization will work together to deliver optimum service to the customer. I believe that a key discipline of the modern, future-fit HR will therefore be in the area of dynamic work architecture and design, well beyond the era of organization charts, grading structures and job descriptions.

Once the work design and workforce planning aspects are thought through, the rest of the talent life-cycle processes need to kick in and align. For example, recruiting for the right skills also needs to account for likely and possible changes in skills requirements further down the line. Attracting people, therefore, with the right attitude and a learning mindset in the knowledge that their immediate skills will change will become increasingly important. Training and development will need to be continuous and provided through a mix of mobile, online, on-the-job, and formal methods that align with changing business needs, as well as different learning styles of a modern workforce on the move.

The continued evolution of the new employment deal and the fragmented nature of the employment landscape described in **Chapter 5** will have a profound effect on talent management and HR strategy in the future. Traditional ways of recruiting, developing and rewarding staff have already been disrupted and are giving way to new ways of acquiring, rewarding, developing and retaining talent. Rewards will be more flexed and individual, with a "consumer grade" employment experience demanded by different generations of employees.

Rapidly emerging technologies and applications provide skills and talent platforms to help employers and employees alike keep on top of the skills revolution and assist in shaping careers. Even how employees exit the organization is changing. Employers are seeing their alumni network as a viable talent pool for the future and/or social advocates for the organization after they leave.

Meanwhile, the physical (and virtual) workplace is changing rapidly, accelerated into the mainstream undoubtedly by the COVID-19 crisis, and it will continue to evolve to accommodate new ways of leading and engaging staff, with remote/blended working models and team working/collaboration becoming the norm.

Central to this new talent management story is a clear picture of the organization's desired culture. There is a risk that some employers will promise the earth to attract sought-after employees only for those new hires to find the employer cannot (or, worse, will not) deliver on its promises. New work models, emerging technology, and skill requirements will change the employment prospects for those employees and their jobs over time. What is the organization's strategy for dealing with this transition in a responsible and ethical way?

Navigating the new strategic HR, talent management, and employment model realities will present both challenges and opportunities for HR and is also a shared challenge with the wider business. Part of the solution must therefore be a re-think of the HR operating model and what we expect from our leaders and front-line managers (and employees themselves). This includes the question of what qualities leaders need to succeed, which will possibly be very different from the qualities organizations have hired and trained for in the past, as we have explored in earlier chapters. As explored in **Chapter 6**, leadership of this new employment landscape, in a sustainable and ethical way, will be central to every HR strategy and approach.

Adoption and application of emerging technology

Rather than being anywhere close to a mature stage in its history, digital transformation is still in its infancy. Writer Yuri van Geest and others have charted out the exponential (*versus* linear) rates of progression of different "convergent" technologies, such as drones, industrial printing, robotics, and cybernetics, over the last decade. The human and organizational implications of these advancements will continue to be profound. Every week brings further discussion and mounting evidence regarding the threats and opportunities posed by the digital age to jobs and employment.

Research from Gartner, a leading global advisory company, established that the organizational, change management, and human impact of digital transformation is as much as 15 times the technological impact caused in digital transformation. Yet over two-thirds of leadership questions and attention have been directed at the technological change agenda. The message that digital transformation is less about technology than it is about people seems to finally be getting through. Again, this poses both opportunity and challenge for HR.

Perhaps the unlikely coalition between IT and HR is just one of the consequences, as the two functions work to maximize the current and future talent agenda for rapidly changing business conditions and needs. Until recently, HR and IT have tended to live very separate lives in the corridors of traditional organizations, both looking rather skeptically and suspiciously at each other across the fence. But as we continue into this digital age, they will need each other more and more. Although responsible for very different disciplines in people and technology, HR and IT are essentially both tasked with helping an organization:

- Deliver on its core business requirements in the short term: its "**run** role;"

- Develop capacity to deliver into the near future: its "**grow** role;"
- Be a transformative function in terms of building either the people or technology environment for the organization to adapt and change into the future and the longer term: its "**transform** role."

HR will look to technology to deal with an ever-growing agenda that is hungry for real-time people data, analytics, digital enablement and automation of key processes, an increasingly digital employee experience, and technology-based efficiencies. IT will look to its HR colleagues to deal with the range of people and cultural challenges triggered by the increasing digital transformation agenda on its plate. IT also needs HR to partner in the skills agenda to access the skills when and where they are needed in an increasing variety of ways.

Another aspect of how these functions can complement each other is in the basic requirement of getting complex work done in a rapidly changing environment as described in **Chapter 2**. IT has been faced with that challenge since Internet-based technologies burst onto the scene in the mid to late 1990s, suddenly sending customer and investor expectations through the roof in the design and delivery of new and existing services. The exponential rise in expectations from IT regarding pace of delivery, complexity, and product or service functionality challenged the traditional way IT had been gradually developing over the previous 50 years. Work innovations, such as the *Agile Manifesto* and other developments, spawned a new era for getting work done in IT over the last 20 years.

HR is at a similar juncture where traditional "plan and control" ways of getting transactional and transformational work done are simply unsustainable. Those old ways of running HR processes no longer meet the demands of an expectant workforce and shifting business leadership priorities.

Digital transformation is less about technology than it is about people.

Given these present realities, it's no surprise that the application of agile methods and practices has taken off at record pace over the last five to 10 years. Both HR and IT now have to navigate a way of working that delivers consistency and reliability but is also open to high levels of flexibility, adaptiveness, and responsiveness. Navigating this paradox is essentially what agility is all about. And HR needs agility to deliver its own services as well as to help enable agility throughout the organization – rather than block it with unnecessary red tape and administrative overload.

David Cagney, Chief Human Resources Officer for the Irish Civil Service, noted:

We need to move to a more dynamic and trust-based regime where HR policy is framed for the compliant majority rather being overly prescriptive, and based on the risk of breach by the deviant few.

Increased complexity, uncertainty and change

As we have seen, when you peel back the layers to get at what really matters in future-proofing our organizations and workforces, one of the main realities we face is a combination of increased complexity, uncertainty, and pace of change. This requires a clear shift from the traditional plan and control ways of working to more dynamic, customer-oriented and, constantly changing approaches to getting work done within – and increasingly outside – our organizations.

This challenge presents several tough choices and knotty dilemmas for business leaders and in particular for business support functions such as IT, Finance and HR, which over time have been charged with controlling activities, compliance, managing risk, and so on. With increased complexity and a broadening mandate, HR is recognizing the "new deal" emerging, and, with it, a heightened responsibility for creating a positive employee experience. It is also looking for where it can add more value by creating the right ecosystem for managers and employees to manage processes and create the experience rather than feeling compelled to map out every process step. Some examples of this shift are:

- Not taking on the responsibility of administering and delivering training but focusing on the creation of the learning organization culture, environment, and support system for employees and leaders to play the lead role in future-proofing their skills and careers;

- Creating an ecosystem and coaching culture so that people can adapt within their own means and with the support of those they work closely with and for – and to not be reliant on formal HR processes and programs;

- Policies are adaptive and written with the trustworthy majority in mind, rather than the deviant few;

- Building a culture of trust, enablement and empowerment – the essence of the new "social contract".

This mindset and approach, supported by enabling technology, is helping to take the burden of expectation to "organize and deliver" people process activity off HR's shoulders. Employee growth and adaptiveness is a shared goal and responsibility, with managers and employees themselves playing their part in a more mature employment deal. HR's value will be as a facilitator and catalyst leader of this system. Its expertise will be seeing the gaps and filling them with the right support rather than rushing to solve every staff problem itself.

HR enabling agility

The underlying capability of agility has been a common thread in the discussion on shaping the Future of Work, embracing the digital age, and dealing with ongoing complexity and change, as was discussed at some length in **Part One** of this book. And, as has been referenced, the manufacturing and technology sectors have been particularly impacted by this "adapt or die" challenge in more recent times. Coping with rapid change and the need for continuous agility has led to several quantum leaps in how work is designed and organized. For example, the *Agile Manifesto* developed in 2001, signaled a shift away from the traditional "waterfall" approach to delivering software products and services commonly used up to that time.

I recall, when researching this field a few years back, wondering whether the agile message or approach had reached the shores of HR or was still the preserve of the technology-oriented functions – as it had been for many years. This is when I came across the work of pioneers in this space such as Pia-Maria Thorén who, in 2017, wrote her first book on the relationship between Agile and HR called *Agile People: A Radical Approach for HR and Managers*. More recently, I had the pleasure of joining Pia-Maria and 34 other authors from the global Agile HR community in writing *Agile Principles: Your Call to Action for the Future of Work*. This community, along with other leaders in the field such as Natal Dank and Fabiola Eyholzer, illustrated that Agile HR has been growing and evolving as a key enabling development for the profession for some time. From my experience to date, it seems to hold some sensible and helpful answers to the challenges posed to HR by the fast-moving and changing world of work.

Thought leader Ahmed Sidky introduced a helpful framework back in 2010 for summarizing the Agile approach in general, which can also be applied to HR. Sidky's approach suggests that we must first consider the idea of the agile mindset, which represents an *openness* to disrupting how HR work gets done. It requires letting go of some of the sacred cows and assumptions of the past. Second, it is about a set of values and principles that guide *how* to do HR work, such as putting more emphasis on the customer/business relationship, collaboration, co-creation, experimentation, iteration, outcome orientation, delegation, and so on. Third, it is about adopting new practices and tools to help execute HR in a different way – both within HR itself and, crucially, with the organization.

Table 7.1: Traditional HR *versus* Agile HR

TRADITIONAL HR (from)	AGILE HR (to)
Prescriptiveness and control	Adaptability (menu) and facilitative
Jobs and roles	Work and skills (machine, human, external/internal)
Politics, rules and standards	Supporting flexibility, speed and collaboration, trust
Deliver programs to customers	Co-create with customers in design and delivery
Technical precision	Experimentation and iteration

But what does Agile HR look like in practice when compared to more traditional HR practices and approaches? **Table 7.1** illustrates the overall contrast between traditional HR and Agile HR, in this case originated by Pia-Maria Thorén and the Agile People community. As in previous tables contrasting traditional and more agile practice in this book, it is not the case that traditional practices are necessarily "bad" but we will see the demand for more reliance on the Agile HR approach in the future as we encounter greater complexity and speed of change.

As those who have developed their practices in this way will tell you, there are two broad applications of Agile HR:

- How can we bring agility and agile practices into running HR?
- How can HR enable agility in the wider organization?

Agility enabling HR

Agility enabling HR is when the function (or any function) examines disciplines and methods for improving how it increases its impact and productivity. Popular disciplines include the Agile movement, Design Thinking and Lean. Learning from the technology, manufacturing, and design worlds, HR can adapt these principles, tools, and practices for its own use. As Pia-Maria Thorén says:

> *HR can either support or hinder organizational agility, which is why it should itself go first in adopting agile principles and practices.*

Let's look at a few examples:

- In recruitment, Agile HR uses methods like Lean and Kanban to map out and visualize the overall process, unlock bottlenecks, and optimize flow as a team;
- For onboarding, HR employs techniques from other disciplines, such as user experience and design thinking, to improve the overall employee experience;
- For activities like job design, compensation, processes, and complex projects, utilization of agile approaches can reduce lead times and vastly improve transparency, bottlenecks, and customer engagement and ownership.

Armed with a better understanding of agility and agile principles, HR can engage with and enable the wider business to improve key people and process challenges. For example, when it comes to the difficult and problematic area of performance management, agile organizations facilitated by HR, tackle the issue head on, using targeted, outcome-oriented methods such as Scrum and Design Thinking, experimentation, and iteration with HR co-creating appropriate performance and feedback processes *with* the business rather than designing it for the business. As Otti Vogt, COO and Chief Transformation Officer C&G at ING, and others point out, classic performance management and other such traditional administrative and command and control processes are prime targets for reform as they stifle rather than enable agility.

With a greater understanding of business, team, and process agility, HR can also play a critical role in supporting the business with its own agility challenges. I recall working with a company on its digital and agility strategy. It was clear that, at the business team level, there were good signs of success. Local teams were developing new, dynamic ways of working, restructuring themselves, and delivering quicker and faster to their customers than ever before. But at a wider organizational level, the business teams were battling against a headwind of traditional management structures and cumbersome HR policies that were slowing them down. And at the individual level, some team leaders and employees needed support to adapt more agile work practices. For some team members, it was a significant shift from what they had learned and from what had been successful for them in the past. This analysis created a clear people agenda for HR to solve specific agility "pain points" with the business teams, particularly in relation to agility-enabling people practices, skills needs and organization design. They were then seen as partners in enabling greater agility in the organization rather than being perceived as removed from the business and administering processes that were, in some cases, blocking agility.

For an organization to be truly digital, agile, and future-fit, HR needs to be front and center.

Clearly, for an organization to be truly digital, agile, and future-fit, *HR needs to be front and center* to make it happen. HR controls or influences so many of the people practices in an organization: from culture, to talent, to contracting and resourcing, to reward, and performance management. And there is ample evidence from my own experience alone that, if HR doesn't take a lead to make people and work practices more "agile friendly," then the business will have no choice but to work around HR – a scenario that could cause even more organizational dysfunction than might have been there in the first place.

One of HR's main challenges is that many of its policies and processes are rooted in the traditional plan and control world of management. Standardization and compliance, for example, have been historically prioritized over flexibility and agility. Ironically, in many cases, this situation has been demand-led from the business leadership, which looked to impose more standardization and one-size-fits-all approaches that work so well in other areas – manufacturing, for example – to corporate people processes and structures.

So, HR is facing somewhat of a crossroads. Does it continue to deliver "as is," just tweaking around the edges enough to get by? Or does it look to a more dynamic mindset and approach that acknowledges and embraces increasing complexity and the pace of change? Does it really have a choice? Fabiola Eyholzer, CEO of Just Leading Solutions, puts it this way:

HR is becoming a key driver of Business Agility. But we cannot get there by incrementally improving the status quo *because the* status quo *itself is built on an outdated view and understanding of the world of work.*

Critically, Agile HR is about working with the business itself, enabling teams to be more agile in how *they* work. Collaborating with them to understand their business flows, adapt key people processes as necessary, and to remove blockages – and then, to just get out of the way.

For some organizations and HR leaders, Agile HR is simply the way they naturally approach HR, and it's nothing new. For most others, it's going to be a longer process to unwind years of traditional assumptions and approaches to how the function is envisioned, executed, and even valued by the business.

What is the advice from others who have travelled this path? Most suggest to first commit to adopting the mindset involved. Then, start small, perhaps with something that will bring an immediate impact to the HR team and their customers. This will help HR leaders gain confidence and demonstrate results.

Unless circumstances demand otherwise, there may not be the need to rush in and disrupt everything all at once. Perhaps some areas of the HR life-cycle will have better potential for this approach than others; and perhaps some processes should even stay as they are in the plan and control world.

Pick your battles. But even if it's messy at first (and it will be) stick with the overall agile principles and mindset: be open, learn from experience, build from success (and failure), and move forward.

Case in Point 7.1: Bol.com

Background

Needing to respond adequately to exponential growth, Bol.com took an innovative approach to involving employees to adapt its structures and ways of working. Moving to a model of self-organizing teams and network structures, the company has transformed how it operates, continuously and openly learning as it goes.

Key Take-aways

o The process began with an experiment, which was carried out on a team of 40, to adopt Bol's version of holacracy called "Spark."

o The team was given the freedom to experiment with how it approached work through new meeting structures and organizational roles.

o Increasing productivity and overall satisfaction among participants of this experiment got them to talk about this new way of working with their colleagues *via* internal communication channels and presentations.

o As more teams started to adopt "Spark," their overall satisfaction was measured through a Net Promoter Score (NPS).

o A low NPS mark allowed the company to provide support to those struggling to get onboard and address issues immediately. This encouraged the new way of working to "go viral" within the organization.

o 300 non-IT employees then joined this new way of working, with more and more teams on the way to adopt "Spark."

o The company also openly acknowledges where teams sometimes find it difficult to start out on the Spark journey but, after a few weeks, the new habits and routines take hold, boosted by the early results and positive wins that the group experience. Critical to that "messy" transition has been the strong purpose-led approach, open leadership and psychological safety provided for what they are trying to achieve – and why.

Sources

https://corporate-rebels.com/bol/.
https://www.linkedin.com/pulse/from-spark-fireworks-first-18-months-change-bolcom-harm-jans/.

Where do we go from here?

Whether the context is Future of Work, digital transformation, shaping post-pandemic work models, globalization, the shifting nature of our relationship with work in the 21st century, or a combination of all of the above, there is no doubt that HR is looking at another major shift on its axis. This shift will be similar, in focus and depth, to the shifts described in our mini HR history tour earlier in the chapter.

HR has a critical role in enabling organizational agility and adaptiveness and in shaping this thing we call the Future of Work. Managing the shift from traditional HR to a more agile approach starts with an appreciation of the exciting, ambitious, and proud leadership role the function has in shaping the Future of Work.

The details of the shape, size, and organization of the function will emerge and develop as each HR team evolves its ways of working and creating value, in partnership with (rather than in service to) its colleagues across the business.

But a mindset check or "reset" is the first crucial factor for HR to succeed in that leadership role and mandate into the future. This exciting time for the profession will allow its participants to help future-proof the working lives of countless people across the globe.

What you can do
On the individual level:

- What do you personally see as the opportunities and challenges for the workforce of the future?
- How will this change impact on your role and what can you do about it?

Case in Point 7.2: BuJo

Background

From the beginning, the BuJo burger restaurant has been passionate about its purpose, values-based culture, and in creating a unique employee experience. While entering a well-served sector, it set about creating new standards of excellence in its business operating model, technology enablement, sustainability, food production and quality, and customer experience. Central to the journey were its people, with the primacy of the stakeholder ranking going from employee to customer to the shareholders – in that order.

Key Take-aways

o   In a crowded market, BuJo has managed to carve out a unique brand and niche by establishing an online, community-based, innovative and physical fast casual restaurant presence.

o   Its care and attention to the people agenda has been clear from the start in how it carefully recruited its first wave of employees and in other initiatives such as setting up a future focused HR operating model

o   As it expanded, the company wanted to ensure the unique and open BuJo culture was integrated into the full people management life-cycle from recruitment through to development, reward, teamwork, leadership capability (at all levels) and other people processes.

o   Adoption of the most progressive people management processes in its sector, embracing Future of Work developments and technologies in people management and ensuring that BuJo stands out in terms of its people culture and operating model as much as it does for its food, technology, and customer experience.

o   The attention to the people brand of its business also has yielded dividends in its staff loyalty, advocacy, community reputation and productivity.

Sources

https://lovindublin.com/lifestyle/dublin-restaurant-in-lovely-gesture-for-older-people-looking-to-dispose-of-their-christmas-trees.
https://shop.bujo.ie/pages/about.

- How do you think this era should be remembered in terms of work and how HR influenced the world of work?

On the organizational level:

- Looking into the Fourth Industrial Age and the Future of Work for your organization, what do you see as the opportunities and challenges for HR?
- What needs to change for HR to grow and respond to your organization's specific challenges and opportunities in the changing world of work?
- What do you think are the benefits and challenges of greater organizational agility for HR?
- What would be different for HR in comparison to more traditional approaches to how HR is managed and run?
- What ways can you see HR benefiting from bringing more agility and agile practices into HR?
- What ways can you see HR supporting and enabling greater agility in the wider organization?

Chapter 8

ORGANIZATIONAL AGILITY – A SYSTEM PERSPECTIVE

Never doubt that a small group of thoughtful,
committed, citizens can change the world.
Indeed, it is the only thing that ever has.

Margaret Mead

I have been a Liverpool soccer club fan for as long as I can remember. As a small boy, my eldest brother had us huddled around a small transistor radio that picked up a poor, long wave BBC radio signal, tuned into the commentary of epic European cup games in the 1970s. And that was it: a life-long loyalty was born to a team from a foreign city I had never seen. After Liverpool had enjoyed huge success in the 1970s and 1980s, nearly 30 years of relative frustration and disappointment followed. But in 2020, Liverpool finally won the English Premiership, and held the titles of English, European, and World club champions in a single year.

What has this story got to do with future ready, agile organizations? The main point is not about agility *per se*, although of course, that plays its part. It is more about what Liverpool's story can teach us about organizational success in competitive and unpredictable environments.

While a wealthy club in relative terms, Liverpool is not *the* wealthiest. Most observers accept that there was something else going on that contributed to its success aside from resources. Was it the charisma and tactics of the manager, Jurgen Klopp; the never-say-die captain on the pitch, Jordan Henderson; the exceptional players on the team; the backroom staff; the talent scouts and deal-makers; the boardroom; the fans? In truth, it was all of these, with everyone together aligned at the same time around a singular purpose and to achieve a special result in the club's history.

Agility is *the* critical enabling factor and capability for Future of Work readiness, survival and success.

Part of the binding force that held this multi-disciplinary enterprise together came from Klopp, who urged all of the stakeholders above, at his very first press conference, to change their mindset from "doubt to belief." It was a simple message that triggered a five-year journey of belief, trust, determination and ultimately, victory. Liverpool's success in 2020 is an example of a whole "system" in purposeful alignment. The team of individuals that created that system had the right resources in different areas of the enterprise; it was mobilized and ready at the right time to succeed and deliver outstanding performance.

This book, quite consciously, thus far has focused on the journey of the individual, the business leader, and the HR function in being Future of Work ready through the adoption of agility in both mindset and skillset. This chapter looks at the organizational or "system" perspective and provides a simple but useful approach to consider and analyze the different moving parts through the purpose and lens of achieving improved and sustainable agility.

Key themes and factors

With continuous business change, new technologies, and the changing workforce, it can be bewildering to get on top of the full range of challenges, opportunities, and strategic options presented by the Future of Work at a system or organizational level. An important first step is to filter down all the hype and concentrate on the real and material issues for your own situation.

As explored in earlier chapters (see **Chapter 2** in particular), in both the external market and internal organizational context, there is a constant need to be present and focused on today. At the same time, it is also necessary to be open to likely (and less likely) scenarios beyond the current realities, projections, and demands of the organization so that the business is strategically positioned for the future. This ambidextrous quality at the organizational level follows the pattern we have seen in the individual level throughout this book. The inevitable conclusion is that agility is *the* critical enabling factor and capability for Future of Work readiness, survival and success, not only for individuals, business leaders, and HR teams, but for organizational systems as well.

From the business leaders we interviewed and worked with, two themes consistently arose when it came to organizational agility:

- The need to build mechanisms to test different business scenarios for the future – from incremental change to major disruption (external "sense" perspective);
- The need to stand back and consider the key internal organizational implications, capabilities, and themes – from strategic flexibility to how the organization's culture, structure, and processes are aligned and the type of workforce it needs for the future (internal "respond" perspective).

Whether you take your starting point from a football club – or indeed the ancient tribes, the military, or a bank – the mobilization, allocation, distribution, and organization of work towards a common cause or purpose is in constant flux and has developed over the years. Ultimately, living with complexity and the speed of change comes down to deliberate choices about how the organization will compete, operate, and adapt, and its overall purpose in doing so.

In *Reinventing Organizations*, Frederic Laloux goes beyond the concept of agility, distinguishing different types of organizations and recognizing the evolutionary shift within them, impacted by societal changes and evolving ways of working. He popularized the concept of the Teal Organization, for example, as the ultimate, purpose-driven, self-managed organizational model, exemplified by organizations such as Viisi and Buurtzorg, highlighted in earlier Case Studies. For simplicity here, we focus on the similar core concept of an agile organization in order to explore the ultimate question of what organizational agility is in real terms and what it looks like.

Figure 8.1: Systemic Agility at Organizational, Team and Individual Levels

Considering the established elements and moving parts associated with organizational agility and adaptiveness, we have combined the various influencing factors of agility that clearly work at four distinct levels in an organization. **Figure 8.1** offers an illustrative strategic framework for agility, based on the key themes encountered in our research and our consulting work.

Agility experts such as Linda Holbeche, the Business Agility Institute, Trish Gorman, and others, have created more sophisticated and detailed models but the one shown here is designed to provide a simple way to identify the key influencing factors and levels associated with organizational agility. At the organizational or systemic level, agility has several layers that need to be considered as a whole and individually. The question is: What can you do to understand how all these moving parts are functioning both independently and as a collective expression of organizational agility?

SCOPE – A model for organizational agility

To assist our clients with this question – and to identify the systemic enablers and blockers of organizational agility – we designed the SCOPE diagnostic process (**Figure 8.2**).

It is a simple and pragmatic tool for organizations that seek to explore, understand, and improve their agility. Under the key headings of Strategy, Culture, Organization, People and External Focus, SCOPE captures the critical business, organizational, and cultural dimensions of organizational agility. It reveals how agility shows up in an organization at a high level where leaders, management, and employees can readily recognize and evaluate the enablers and blockers of their current level of agility and future-state requirements.

Figure 8.2: The SCOPE Model

S. ⟶ **STRATEGY**
How is Agility positioned and demonstrated
in the organization's strategy?

C. ⟶ **CULTURE + LEADERSHIP**
To what extent does culture and leadership
behaviour support agile habits and practices?

O. ⟶ **ORGANIZATION**
How do the organization's structures, processes
and technology enable agility or get in its way?

P. ⟶ **PEOPLE**
Do the workforce planning, talent and people
management processes support or block agility?

E. ⟶ **EXTERNAL FOCUS**
Does the organization scan the external
environment, sense changes and partner
to enable innovation and flexibility?

The objective of SCOPE is to facilitate open discussion and discovery. It is not an attempt to over-simplify the complexities of an organization, or its agility initiatives, down to a few sound bites, or a naïve, one-size-fits-all consultant's model. It is simply intended to enable a structured walk through the research-based themes that need to be surfaced and addressed by leaders and teams when considering organizational agility.

The SCOPE Model, or organizational agility "health check," consists, in its shorter, form of a 14-statement diagnostic process and online questionnaire. The statements used as a basis to explore the six themes are summarized in the SCOPE tool in **Figure 8.3**.

Figure 8.3: A SCOPE Agility Assessment (Summary)

	Organizational Agility Statement
S	> Agility and adaptiveness are explicitly called out and expressed in our strategy as priorities across the whole business. > Agile principles, like Customer engagement, Changeability, Collaboration, etc., strongly influence our business planning processes.
C	> We have an agile culture throughout the organization – there is a supportive culture of experimentation, co-creation and innovation for the benefit of our customers. > There is a an open and trusting environment across our organization where innovation, continuous learning and even failure is encouraged. > Leaders of our organization take accountability, trust employees and enable a culture of experimentation and learning by doing – they themselves follow agile practices and behaviors.
O	> Our organizational structure enables agile practices and outcomes like cross-functional working, collaboration and networking. > Our systems and technology enable agile decision-making and outcomes such as real-time business data insights, digital flexibility and customer intelligence and metrics. > Our operational processes tend to adapt quickly, taking into consideration the changes happening in the external business environment. > We have agile team structures and processes in place that help us efficiently organize and prioritize our work, flex resources and work across team boundaries. > Our decision-making processes are flexible and can vary depending on the needs of specific initiatives; they are consciously distributed and delegated throughout the organization.
P	> Our workforce planning, recruitment, talent management and deployment processes are designed with workforce agility and flexibility in mind. > Our HR processes and policies (training, reward, performance and recognition, etc.) are recognized as important enablers of workforce and organizational agility.
E	> We optimize external partnerships and relationships in our business operating model (co-creation of value with suppliers and external partners). > Our organization takes steps to deliberately scan the internal and external environment to identify opportunities and risks for our business.

Rate your organization using these scales – and identify any gaps.
Current State Score: 1. Disagree; 2. Somewhat disagree; 3. Unknown / undecided; 4. Somewhat agree; 5. Agree
Importance to Business: 1. Not important; 2. Somewhat important; 3 Unknown / undecided; 4. Important; 5. Very important

The tool then provides a platform for an important conversation as to the current and target state of agility for any organization (see **Figure 8.4**). The process then typically surfaces other questions and areas of discovery and attention required. Business and HR leaders can work on it with their teams to identify the strengths, challenges, enablers, and blockers of agility unique to their organizations.

Figure 8.4: A Sample of SCOPE Output

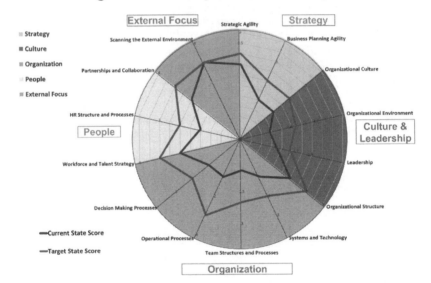

Strategy

Organizational agility is a common theme that emerges from any review of modern-day strategy or analysis of what is needed to thrive in the Future of Work. We explored this topic in **Chapter 6** when considering strategic agility though the work of people like Rita McGrath and McKinsey's Three Horizons.

If business leaders can improve an organization's agility and build it into their strategy, culture, structure, and processes, they will be better significantly better prepared for future challenges and opportunities. Just look at what Netflix and Amazon have done with their business models over the last 10 years.

Organizations that have purpose-driven strategies attract employees who are more engaged, committed, and intrinsically motivated. We explored in earlier chapters how purpose – understood and expressed by organizations but felt and internalized by individuals – is a powerful driver of agility and learning. Furthermore, studies prove that organizations with a clear purpose perform better than those whose purpose is not consistent and clear. Boston Consultancy Group's research, for example, concluded that:

Alignment, clarity, guidance and energy act as fuel to a transformation by providing an emotional connection that inspires greater commitment.

In our research, business leaders confirmed the importance of agility as a conscious organizational strategy rather than a reactive, episodic, or "heroic" trait. Similarly, researchers such as Dr. Ashutosh Muduli further confirm that organizations are adopting agility as a "deliberate" strategy to thrive in an increasingly complex business environment.

In our SCOPE analysis, we ask a few simple questions to gauge to what degree agility is present and prioritized in the organization's strategy. It also explores whether that strategic "intent" is followed through in subsequent business planning processes and decision-making. This can raise some interesting questions – not just within the leadership or the executive team – but amongst the senior team and lower levels of management and employees, too. If agility is not recognizable, present, or being lived in the expression of an organization's strategic execution, how can it be a serious priority in day-to-day behavior and decision-making?

Culture

Culture eats strategy for breakfast, as Peter Drucker famously said. It is certainly true in the case of agility where the day-to-day collective habits and behaviors of people in an organization (the culture) are an expression of what is valued, tolerated, and viewed as the acceptable way to do things.

> **Living with complexity and the speed of change comes down to some deliberate choices.**

In simple terms, day-to-day organizational habits and behaviors on the ground will either be conducive to agility or they won't. Are agile behaviors – collaboration, experimentation, innovation, learning, and co-creation – valued? Or is the culture more traditional, siloed, and fixed in terms of its mindset and approach?

In the SCOPE approach, we ask some specific questions about culture to help teams think about the extent to which leaders support, encourage, and role model agile behaviors and practices. The evaluation gives leaders a picture of whether their intent for an agile organization is playing out in the day to day reality of working life in the organization. It also captures their level of ambition for an agile culture and what the gap might be between their current and target state.

Organization

In addition to understanding the strategic and cultural dimensions of organizational agility, it is also critical to understand how the organization is "set up" for agility. The boundaries of traditional organizations are becoming more blurred. The early to mid-20th century model of accommodating all of a business's functions under one roof has given way to an array of outsourcing models and different options to get work done.

Paying attention to the elements within the internal organization allows you to identify your existing formal structures, processes, and systems, and what is needed for the future. In several instances, we witnessed cases where an organization's efforts to be more agile were hampered by traditional power structures, decision-making processes, and inadequate technology.

Otti Vogt, COO and Chief Transformation Officer C&G at ING, should know. An experienced practitioner and global thought leader in building better businesses, he has implemented large-scale business change programs across sectors, and delivered the agile business transformation for ING globally. He observes that the agile transformations he has witnessed around the world often struggle when realities of existing power and ownership structures are not fully addressed. He highlights the need for vertical leadership development, at the top, and the role of "liberating structures" in maturing organizational agency and self-management. Moreover, he points out that traditional people management and financial support processes need a significant overhaul to enable agility and organizational learning at scale. These elements take time. Nevertheless, it is helpful to assess where you are and how your systems and processes either enable or block agility within teams and functions.

People

Traditional organizational structures are being disrupted and alternative, more agile methods of sourcing work and skills are being sought through talent platforms, free agent workers, and other sources. We are moving rapidly towards a more dynamic, hybrid, customer-oriented, and constantly changing approach to work. Skill requirements, ways of working, and ways of learning in jobs and careers are evolving at an increasing rate and in more unpredictable ways.

Case in Point 8.1: ING

Background

ING began an agile journey as part of its ambitious "Think Forward" business transformation. In response to rapidly changing customer needs, technology, regulatory requirements and increasing competition, it sought to build pace and flexibility into its operational model, bridging silos and harnessing global innovation across 40 countries – first in 2015 across business functions in the Netherlands, and in 2017 as an enabler for its global platform strategy.

Key Take-aways

o   In the delivery organization, staff were consolidated into 9-member self-steering teams called "Squads." "Chapters" were responsible for improving knowledge across squads and "Tribes" were a collection of Squads (< 150 people).

o   IT and business colleagues are working together in multidisciplinary squads based on an agile Scrum framework aiming to improve time to market and customer experience, and boost efficiency and engagement.

o   Call centers, operations and sales adopted different agile structures that best suited their way of working.

o   Employees participated in an intense (re-)selection process that not only looked at skills and capabilities of employees, but also at their capability to work as a team. The organization was flattened and many employees changed roles.

o   Support functions such as HR, Risk and Finance changed their way of working to align with the Tribe setup.

o   Changes in governance and organizational culture, fostered by ING's "Orange Code", supported ING's platform strategy and agility at scale

o   Efficiency and global reuse of developments, time to market and ING's NPS significantly improved, while employee engagement is currently amongst the highest in the sector.

Sources

ING's Agile Transformation - https://www.mckinsey.com/industries/financial-services/our-insights/ings-agile-transformation.

Case Study: ING Bank's Digital Platform Tribe Goes Agile - https://cdn.ymaws.com/www.agilebusiness.org/resource/resmgr/documents/casestudy/ing_bank_-_agile_mindset_cas.pdf.

Examining the current and target state of your people/talent strategy and HR processes will help to identify the necessary reforms as well as the required skills for the future workforce, leaders, teams, and functions.

SCOPE specifically enquires about the extent to which:

- Workforce planning and talent management strategies support the development of an agile organization, including utilizing different, diverse worker types and deploying different ways of getting work done (contracting, gig, agency work, and automation);
- HR processes (training, performance management, rewards, etc.) and policies support and enable organizational agility, including work flexibility policies and utilization of remote working practices.

External focus and orientation

This last section of the SCOPE evaluation approach explores the extent to which an organization engages with the external environment:

- Is it effective at sensing and scanning for potential opportunities and threats?
- Is it open and curious regarding innovation and disruption to its own products, services, and how it produces and delivers them?

A breakthrough idea could come from a supplier, a customer, or a competitor. One CEO said to me:

Our aim is to disrupt ourselves based on what we see going on in the market before we get disrupted by someone else.

Case in Point 8.2: Rijksmuseum

Background

When the Rijksmuseum, the national museum of art in the Netherlands, got the opportunity to reinvent itself, it adopted agile practices of collaboration, dissolved and reformed teams to execute this transformation, and continued its long tradition of innovation with its first year seeing over 2.5 million visitors.

Key Take-aways

o Singular specializations like painting, textiles, etc. were abandoned in favor of multi-specialty groups organized by century.

o Tasked with creating a historical narrative, teams worked together to create a long list of items to be showcased at the opening.

o A person who specialized in a century of human history chaired each team. Teams then worked together in a way that worked for them to form consensus and execute their plan.

o Teams were then dissolved and new teams recreated to curate a shortlist of items.

o Success of agile practices ensured they were continued past the opening, which led to a permanent change to the overall organizational structure of the museum.

o Today teams are still created and dissolved to improve the quality of the four main pillars of the organization: exhibitions, personal stories, customer journey, and innovation.

Sources

https://www.synerzip.com/blogs/4-examples-of-agile-in-non-technology-businesses/.

https://www.mckinsey.com/business-functions/organization/our-insights/accidentally-agile-an-interview-with-the-rijksmuseums-taco-dibbits.

So often, we focus on the short-term scope of what we are doing and fail to see the danger or opportunity in the periphery. In the SCOPE evaluation approach, we explore the extent to which this tendency to sense and scan what is going on in the external (and even internal) environment is part of the organization's way of doing things – and what it might do to improve that capability into the future.

Where do we go from here?

Although the approach to organizational agility will be different from case to case, leaders should be in a position to consider and articulate their current and desired level of agility at the "system" level. Whatever the approach used, analysis, assessment and development of organizational agility needs to be adopted as a proactive, strategic priority in the business and HR planning agenda if deliberate progress is to be made in improving agility from a whole system perspective.

Such work will help to continuously raise and maintain awareness on what needs to be done to develop a more sustainable agile culture and capability. The SCOPE model provides one way of beginning that conversation and getting leaders to identify what their agility agenda needs to focus on for their business needs.

What you can do
On the individual level:

- From the perspective of your own role, how would you evaluate the organizational "system" you are part of in terms of its agility? Use the headings and definitions of the SCOPE tool to carry out your own review from your perspective;

- What could you do within your own sphere of influence to increase the organizational agility of your own area? Are there things you could do more of or less of yourself to improve agility in your own "system?" Use the SCOPE criteria to define the current state, to envision the desired future state and to frame a plan.

On the organizational level:

- Using the SCOPE definitions in this chapter (or the versions available from WorkMatters.ie), evaluate how agile your organization is today from an enterprise or system level.
- Using the same criteria, define how agile the organization should be in order to compete in the current and future business or operating environment (target state).
- Ideally, get your colleagues from different levels and areas of the organization to do the same exercise and identify/discuss the key areas of agreement and difference.
- Based on priority areas of concern or opportunity and the extent of the gaps between the current and target state, develop a plan of action to increase your organizational agility in a few high impact areas.

Part Four

A CALL TO ACTION FOR THE FUTURE

Chapter 9

SOCIETAL IMPLICATIONS FOR THE FUTURE OF WORK

Crafting a future that offers broad-based security and prosperity may prove to be the greatest challenge of our time.
Martin Ford

According to Klaus Schwab, Founder and Executive Chairman of the World Economic Forum, the trends explored in this book are bringing us to the point of:

> *... a technological revolution that will fundamentally alter the way we live, work, and relate to one another. In its scale, scope, and complexity, the transformation will be unlike anything humankind has experienced before.*

If this is the case, what will our employment landscape look like in the future? With all this technological firepower and knowledge at our disposal, how can we ensure that we shape the broad-based and prosperous world of work we want to see?

At a macro level, understanding organizational agility and the practical implications of the Future of Work informs the choices we all face as a society – and how we build an ecosystem to support our organizations and how and where we will work in the future – regulations, taxation, educational policy, and more.

Society's role and obligation

Society at large needs to play a proactive role and take more notice of what is really happening in the Future of Work. The design of our collective Future of Work cannot be left *solely* to the corporate world, as it also figures out its own way forward for survival and success in a competitive, global marketplace. How we collectively lead the next phase in areas such as employment policy, education, taxation and job activation will determine – not just impact – the success of our organizations and the quality and very nature of work for generations to come.

This book has purposely focused on the practical actions we can all proactively take as individuals, leaders, and organizations to shape and thrive in the Future of Work. Yet, there are wider questions at play for our politicians, policy-makers, educators and all of us if we are to ultimately meet the challenge posed by Martin Ford in his quote at the top of this chapter.

"Good work"

Amongst all the developments and trends regarding work, it is arguably more important than ever that we go back to basics and reflect on where work itself is going. How are we shaping the world of work for the next generation of workers? What will the ultimate benefit be of all this progress and new technology if it can't improve the economic livelihood of the wider human race, as well as the health and well-being of the planet and her citizens? It seems, at minimum, we must ensure that:

- For those who have work, it is "good and meaningful work" that provides a basis for satisfaction, supporting families, and progressing careers;
- People don't get left behind in the digital, growth-driven race we have created.

The concept of "good work" has been explored in many ways over the years: from the QuInnE model developed by the Institute of Employment Research on what constitutes job quality to David Rock's SCARF (Status, Certainty, Autonomy, Relatedness and Fairness) model, which represents what workers want and need from work. Perhaps a helpful definition that captures the essence of these variants is that from the Chartered Institute of Personnel and Development (CIPD), which suggests that good work:

- Is fairly rewarded;
- Gives people the means to securely make a living;
- Gives opportunities to develop skills and a meaningful career with a sense of fulfillment;
- Provides a supportive environment with constructive relationships;
- Allows for work-life balance;
- Is physically and mentally healthy;
- Gives employees the voice and choice they need to shape their working lives;
- Is accessible to all.

Not an unreasonable list. Just ask the likes of Tom Van der Lubbe of Viisi, Jos de Blok from Buurtzorg, or the founders of BuJo. These visionaries have been creating people-centric, purpose-driven, and autonomous work models in their organizations since they were formed. The importance, value, quality and essence of "ordinary work," including factors such as being purpose-led, engaged, challenged, having social engagement and having a sense of control, growth or empowerment in what you do, is now increasingly recognized. Daniel Pink, as previously referenced, calls out Autonomy, Purpose and Mastery in his book, *Drive*, as central to what employers of any shape and size can provide their workforce without it necessarily costing a penny, and is, in fact, much more likely to demonstrate significant financial and reputational returns.

The definition of good work may be clear enough in theory, but we are clearly struggling to reach those standards in practice, despite a growing number of stories like Viisi, BuJo, Buurtzorg and others. And among those lucky enough to have work, the reality still exists globally of record levels of dis-engagement, stress, and burnout in the workplace. Precarious work arrangements such as zero hour contracts are also on the rise, as are the risks they bring – not just to the health and wellbeing of workers and their families but also to societal cohesion and political stability. You only need to think only of the Rust Belt, Brexit, or economic migration for this ricochet effect to be apparent.

Isn't it also a moral and ethical obligation on all of us to hand over a better world of work to the next generation?

Employers might, for example, take notice from the likes of PayPal and others in considering new pay models that contrast with the old norms – pay models that reflect ideas and values such as "net disposable income" and the living wage rather than just the "market rate" for skills and labor. While employers have a leading role in generating broadly satisfying work though a new employment deal, as we explored in **Chapter 5**, the employee also shares in achieving that goal for themselves. Individuals, as we have explored, need to accept their own role and responsibilities in finding "good work" and adapting to an increasingly disrupted work environment and future.

Research shows time and again that the most engaged and contented workers understand that the tasks they do are part of the big picture of what their job means for themselves, the organization and the customers they serve. Happier workers are able to distinguish between what they *do* and who they *are*; their approach, mindset, and attitude towards work define their satisfaction with their work more than the work itself. Critical to this, whatever the level of the job, is a sense of choice, control, and respect amongst their community. Not every job or company purpose involves saving the world but individuals can go a long way towards feeling that way as a choice. Through its attitude and support, Society can also increase that sense of respect and pride in "ordinary work" as well.

The universal respect and gratitude expressed towards the numerous categories of essential front-line workers during the COVID-19 crisis was an example of the type of support and value society can and should place on "ordinary" and "good" work into the future. While employers have a role in generating broadly satisfying work, the achievement, support, reward, and recognition of good work for the majority of citizens is typically a challenge for wider society in practice.

An understanding of and appreciation for what good work looks like is an important stepping stone as we consider what the Future of Work will be or could be going forward. In *The Why of Work*, Wendy and Dave Ulrich capture the case for meaningful and "abundant" work not just for workers but for organizations, customers and for society at large. We now have greater choice than ever before in how we shape and design work, but don't we all – as employers, policy-makers, investors, and citizens – need to exercise that choice carefully and with consideration for the common good? This creation of a positive, accessible world of work is not just a question of economic commonsense, professional duty or even personal fulfilment – isn't it also a moral and ethical obligation on all of us to hand over a better world of work to the next generation?

For a more fundamental change of attitude (and policy) towards the emerging world of work to develop, a broader coalition in society needs to be behind and committed to the changes we need to see, so that we can collectively persist and prevail through the agitation and uncomfortable, bumpy transition that has historically accompanied every major period of disruption in the world of work over hundreds of years. And, as with everything in this modern era, we need to attend to this transition faster and in a more agile way than we have done as a human race in earlier cycles and centuries.

The investment community's role and responsibility

I recall an interview with a Commercial Director of a company as part of a review of the company's organizational culture. She explained to me that, if I really wanted to understand the company's culture and what was *really* valued, I should just "follow the money and how we spend it"! The familiar truth she was expressing was that the prioritization of capital and resources tells a lot about what is really important and valued in an organization and in wider society.

The old adage of "what gets measured, gets done" holds true when it comes to corporate behavior and priorities. Therefore, the role of the investment community is important in moving organizational commitment and the Future of Work in the right direction. Some measure of progress has been made in recent years concerning the broadening of what investors are looking for in relation to what progressive organizations are doing through their people practices and social responsibility in general. But it has been slow in coming. Dr. Jean Cushen of Maynooth University noted in her research of the historical relationship between corporate "financialization" and labor:

Scholars of financialization conclude that, far from seeking a competitive advantage by investing in people to create productive value, financial markets pressure business leaders to destabilize and extract value from the employment relationship.

Stakeholder capitalism is not a new idea. The approach seeks to prioritize the interests of a broader range of stakeholders and interests, as opposed to just shareholders, which includes employees, suppliers, customers, communities, and even the environment. The concept is enjoying somewhat of a renaissance, after 50 years or more of relatively unbridled prioritization of the shareholder. The momentum seems to be growing for moving beyond the primacy of the shareholder's financial return as the only measure of long-term company value and sustainability.

Larry Fink, CEO of BlackRock, the world's largest asset management firm, points out:

The fact is the best businesses are defined by more than their short-term profitability. They drive broad-based prosperity by creating value for shareholders, customers, employees, and society alike. When they invest in giving employees the most in-demand skills, for instance, it is clearly good for their business.

The World Economic Forum has been championing this area for some time with the proclamation of the *Davos Manifesto*. These developments and the likes of the Business Roundtable initiative have garnered the attention of and some level of commitment from the world's top organizations. These initiatives mark a hopeful change in the attention and commitment of many global employers and leaders towards this alternative and more nuanced view of capitalism, which includes the achievement of a more secure and future-ready world of work for society at large.

According to the Embankment Project for Inclusive Capitalism (EPIC), which is made up of companies, asset managers, and asset owners with approximately $30 trillion of assets under management (at time of writing):

> *If businesses want to prepare for a rapidly changing future, they might want to invest in employee training or innovation programs – even though that means they have lower dividends or short-term profitability. However, without a clear way to measure and communicate to investors why these trade-offs will pay off in the long term, many businesses feel compelled to put them off or avoid them entirely. And when businesses stop investing in the future, our entire economy suffers.*

The author Stephen Denning points out, however, that only time will tell whether investor actions follow the words of good "shop front" intentions. The development of investment frameworks, such as ESG, and an increasing trend towards more holistic corporate measurement and reporting standards do seem to be moving us beyond principled guidelines to harder measures and transparent reporting obligations. The International Standards Organization, for example, in 2019 released a new standard for human capital that includes metrics on ethics, leadership, diversity, health, and culture.

ESG, in particular, has captured the attention of corporate boards and has taken hold as an increasingly important factor in reputational, sustainable, and ethical governance. The Social pillar of the ESG framework includes a focus on progressive labor management and human capital development standards. The global human resources firm, Mercer, has stated that ESG is an increasingly important "workforce strategy" in itself. ESG issues are a significant factor in the decision-making of millennials (born after 1980), Gen Z (born after 1995), and Gen Alpha (born after 2010) workers. These groups are due to account for over 70% of the workforce by 2029. Prospective employees and investors are not the only parties paying increased attention to a company's

ESG agenda. Regulators, procurement, credit rating agencies, lenders, and consumers are paying attention, too. The focus and scrutiny on sustainability and corporate reputation is only set to expand in the future.

Politicians and policy-makers need to lead and align

With the corporate and investment worlds hopefully more aware of, and committed to, the mutual benefits of good and sustainable work, and shifting their axis to a more worker-friendly and future-ready work environment, the question might be asked: What should politicians and policy-makers be doing to create and support the policy and service ecosystem needed for work and workers to thrive?

Policy-makers from education, social welfare/security, enterprise development, taxation, and labor market activation need to proactively engage with the new economic, societal, educational, and labor force implications of the Future of Work environment of the 21st century. In many countries, such as in Ireland, the public policy, education and support systems are still largely oriented towards a permanent, 9am to 5pm, five-day a week employment model. While the "analog" world of full-time and pensionable jobs is giving way to the "digital," dispersed, and more fragmented world of work, our employment and training support systems, Government policy-makers, and public services have yet to catch up. There is a responsibility on the Government and public systems to put a 21st century employment infrastructure and ecosystem in place to support a 21st century work environment.

Greater systemic agility and a more integrated, cross-governmental, and cross-sectoral mindset needs to be introduced into policy planning. This will encourage a more joined-up approach and more effective integration of related and interconnected policy areas. Given that society will need to prepare for different labor market requirements and a more dynamic, fast-moving employment system in the future, this integration will be essential. What is the point of ticking a political box and creating a glossy strategy about, say, the future of education without working with colleagues in other related sectors as to what that strategy contains or means, in practical terms, for related policy areas and how it can be integrated and moved forward? Outcomes – more than outputs – are needed.

> **Every country should have a cross-sectoral, apolitical, and multidisciplinary Future of Work Commission.**

Further discussions on issues such as the "digital dividend" and variations of the "living wage" concept need to be considered against a collaborative, thought-through, joined-up vision for the Future of Work realities. Such factors should be weighed for the long-term, not just on popular political ideology that pops up from time to time, usually when elections are coming up, and then quickly forgotten again.

These imperatives notwithstanding, some excellent work has been done in recent years to promote the principles of good work and integrated Future of Work planning. The Taylor Report on good work in the UK is one example, as is the white paper, *Reimagining Work*, produced by the German Ministry of Labor and Social Affairs in 2015. This latter research was also accompanied by various public information, workshops, and consultation initiatives, most helpful for updated, livable policies for the future. This approach demonstrated that the Future of Work is an important topic or us all to be involved with, not just left to a few policy experts who may furnish a report from time to time for the transitory Government of the day.

A systemic mindset shift is required

The myriad of such reports, ongoing research, and commentary on this subject *versus* what you see play out on the ground reminds me of the individual mindset shift required for the new world of work as explored in **Chapter 3**. A mindset shift is also necessary at the system level to envision and redesign our approach, our models, the supporting structures, and policies towards Future of Work readiness. Despite all the reports mentioned earlier, it still somehow feels like the official systems (employment policy, education, skills, taxation, etc.) are missing the fundamental belief and conviction that making real change requires. A wholesale systemic mindset shift will help us, as a society, to really move towards the new target state we intellectually know is right to prepare for the times ahead.

Even though we see the rapid evolution of work happening around us, our infrastructure and polices are still trapped in the old world of work paradigm rooted in the traditional, 20th century model of work. We flirt with the ideas and strategies eloquently presented in well-meaning and intellectually compelling reports, like Taylor, but when it then comes to sustainable action and a genuine paradigm shift for the future, the moment passes in favor of the next short term priority. We default back to the more familiar perceptions and short-term mental models about work. We then narrow our focus to tweaking the policy systems we already have and being satisfied with just inching forward. This approach risks leaving countless workers behind, as they struggle to keep up with the educational and skill requirements of the future while the world of work leaps ahead.

Just as we are asking employers, leaders, and workers to adopt and commit to a Future of Work mindset, the same applies to our politicians and policy-makers. If a genuine belief and conviction to move this agenda forward is absent, little will change. We will continue to tweak around the edges of our existing systems –

whether in relation to jobs policy, education, or social security reform – and will be ill-equipped for Future of Work realities.

Future of Work commissions
To help move the agenda forward and to build momentum, a commitment to action towards the direction we seek needs to be made. Obviously, shifts in public mood and policy take time but, as a minimum action step, every country should construct a cross-sectoral, apolitical, and multidisciplinary Future of Work Commission charting the specific way forward for that country. Citizens at large need a clear, fully debated, balanced vision and picture of what the future world of work looks like for themselves and their children. Perhaps, prompted by COVID-19 and the spirit of reimagining the world of work for the 21st century, such a commission could create long-term, integrated solutions for Future of Work readiness and design that are applicable and suitable for their specific country and economy. The political system (regardless of its make up) should then be mandated and public servants empowered to take those proposals forward, and integrate them with other priorities and reform programs of the day. Broad-based national consensus on the direction of travel should be established to sustain clear, consistent and longer-term, systemic change that would persist well after the lifetime of any particular Government's term in office, so that progress in the right direction is sustained.

Back to the future
Observers of the evolving world of work point to other times in history when a significant change in the underlying economic and technological landscape has triggered far-reaching impact and a clear step-change on how we work and live. For example, the changes implicit in the Third Industrial Revolution, brought about by advances in computer technology during the last quarter of the

20th century, resulted in what has been dubbed by Gerald Davis, author of *The Vanishing American Corporation*, the "Nikefication" of work. In this model, the organization is no longer a single entity where work is done. Instead, it is a global ecosystem of inter-connected partners and suppliers. The term implies the overall outsourcing of production and distribution, often internationally.

The more recent "Uberization" of work, in the Fourth Industrial Revolution, signaled the re-emergence from history of the free agent – in the form of the contingent or gig worker – as part of a distributed work model. Introducing the inherent risks and benefits associated with it, these changes have already reshaped the world of work as we knew it to be during the latter half of the 20th century.

Coming just 10 years after the financial crisis, a global pandemic again reminded us how fragile employment is in a service-dominated, inter-connected, and rapidly changing economy. COVID-19 simply accelerated the thinking, trends, and practices regarding innovative and remote ways of working. It further challenged assumptions about how, and where, and by whom work can be done. Keeping with the (questionable) pattern of identifying shifts in the world of work by naming it after leading US multinationals, it could be said that the COVID-19 pandemic solidified the "Zoomification" of work, which quickly arrived as a mainstream, normal way of doing business. Video conferencing, remote working, and online collaboration were no longer restricted to the particular sectors and work cultures where they had already existed for many years. Only time will tell what this Zoomification of work will mean for employers and workers as we shape the new world of work.

Ironically, could the pandemic be seen by history as the "circuit breaker" that was needed to slow the runaway train of the Fourth Industrial Revolution that we have characterized in this book?

Rather than continuously *reacting* to the latest trends and futile attempts to go faster and faster, maybe we can look back at this moment as a time when we *responded* instead; when we were *forced* to pause, to take full advantage of that small and precious "space between stimulus and response," as Viktor Frankl put it. Perhaps this period will lead to a more human-centric and authentic world of work and set the tone for the future so that people can thrive at work rather than struggle just to keep up? Perhaps it will force us into a more mature employment relationship, built on the principles of a new employment deal – genuine partnership, empathy, trust, and broad-based security – and lead to a world where technology will deliver on its promise of flexible working lives and free us from the more inflexible work practices of the 20th century. Will the next phase of progress be about generating good work and broad-based prosperity rather than fueling the earlier priorities such as optimizing technological advancements to create maximum economic efficiency, growth, and financial return?

While commentators will correctly point out the dangers ahead, there are many positive signs for the Future of Work. We have never had so much information, technology, and talent at our disposal. We have a new generation of informed and confident workers more likely to influence, demand, and shape positive change than their predecessors.

We have numerous examples of progressive employment practices demonstrated by inspiring business and HR leaders around the globe (some referenced in this book but far too many to mention). There are signs of positive action being taken by key stakeholders such as investors and those responsible for policy development – and strong voices ready to ensure no one is left behind. With all this talent and these resources at our disposal, what will the history books say about the world of work that *we all* created in the first half the 21st century?

Chapter 10

YOUR CALL TO ACTION IN SHAPING THE FUTURE OF WORK

If you want to change the future, you must change what you're doing in the present.
Mark Twain

This book's journey began with a simple but clear logic summarized in the **Foreword** by Dave Ulrich:

1. The future is uncertain with disruption to working life coming at us with increased frequency, speed, and scale than ever before.

2. Harnessing uncertainty requires the core capability of agility.

3. Agility needs to be properly understood, considered, and developed over multiple settings:
   - Strategic agility;
   - Organizational and team agility;
   - Leadership agility;
   - Individual agility.

4. In shaping the Future of Work and a new employment landscape, HR can enable and institutionalize agility.

5. Cultivating an agile mindset at the individual level ultimately goes to the heart of the Future of Work and the change journey ahead for all of us. It also needs to be developed and expressed at a wider societal and policy context as well.

An objective of this book has been to highlight the work, talent, and leadership of others who have already ventured down this Future of Work path. Their insights and stories of what the Future of Work already looks like provide us with a rough map to find our own way. Their leadership and example give us a sense of direction and confidence that ultimately, everything will be OK when it comes to such an important aspect of our lives – the work we do and why we do it. Their stories and ideas are living proof that we can create and thrive in an exciting and empowering Future of Work rather than merely survive, cope, and get by.

Through working in this field over many years and helping others navigate the practical implications of the changing world of work, I have always been struck by the words of William Gibson we first visited in **Chapter 1**:

The future is already here, it is just unevenly distributed.

The phrase has been picked up and used for many purposes, including raising the question of equity and inequality, especially in regard to how the benefits gained in our future are fairly distributed. In our context, it also reminds us to observe and to be open to the examples and experiences of those who seem to thrive in a fast-moving, ever-changing world of work.

In all the consulting and training work we do, with teams and individuals, helping to break down the Future of Work topic into practical implications and next steps, the same question always arises: What can I do about it now, in the short-term, when I still have so many other shorter-term priorities and demands to also consider? Like the skiing and agility analogy from **Chapter 2**, how can I focus on and navigate the obstacles directly in front of me, while also scanning, sensing, and adapting to the wider, and constantly changing landscape around me?

Five steps towards your Future of Work

To create some momentum in your Future of Work journey, five simple and actionable steps come to mind, each adopted by many fellow "Future of Work shapers and activists" around the world:

- Dream big, start small and start now;
- Peer groups and networks;
- Get the support you need;
- Source the right talent and let them figure it out;
- Adopt an agile mindset.

Dream big, start small and start now

Recalling the momentum building steps outlined in **Chapter 3** of setting a purposeful direction, taking positive action, and adapting and learning, Future of Work builders always highlight the necessity to start and try something with a clear vision and purpose, even if it's simply a small project or a self-development goal. It could be a prompt from one of the action steps recommended at the end of each chapter in this book. Pick one or two that resonate with you or your team at work. Focus on an action that will be of benefit and that will create self-sustaining and purpose-serving insights and learning for you.

The organizations we have worked with and studied have always learned and benefited from setting up small teams or simply encouraged individuals to explore "Horizon 3" topics, themes (as introduced in **Chapter 6**), and possible developments for the business that are more in the periphery than straight ahead. Such explorations could lead to experiments and innovations that will benefit the future of the firm. And the outcome of such initiatives, while welcome, is not necessarily the end goal in itself. Rather, the more enduring and meaningful outcome is what such initiatives say and prove about the culture, openness, and mindset of organizations that facilitate discovery and individual empowerment towards creating a better future.

Taking the opportunity to shape the world of work towards a better future following a major disruption is also an effective way to make a step change that would otherwise be difficult in "normal" times. Creating new, post-pandemic work models and arrangements, for example, presents a once in a lifetime opportunity to practice the principles proposed in this book and to literally design the Future of Work in front of our own eyes. The few years following the pandemic, with its particular impact on the world of work, is unusual compared to other major economic disruptions where *both* employers and employees are *together* expecting and seeking quite radical changes to how and where work is done. Both sides are also expecting a period of experimentation and trial and error as very different work models are developed. Take such opportunities to embed agility and Future of Work readiness and run with it.

Peer groups and networks
One of the clear messages coming from all the research and practice of navigating complexity – as well as effective adaptive, innovative, and agile working – is the importance of accessing and cultivating collaborative networks. These can be formal or informal, external, and internal; just "places" where you can co-create and learn from a diverse, but purpose-driven, group of peers to validate and challenge your ideas and plans for the future.

Future of Work leaders get this, as indicated above, and they encourage a culture of informal and formal networks to span boundaries and to thrive around the firm. Increasingly when an organization hires someone, they are hiring them for who they know and what access they might bring to the wider ecosystem in which the company operates. Internally, we in WorkMatters, and the folks in the Agile People community, help organizations to build cross-functional "buddy groups." Such groups are set up deliberately for a specific purpose or mission, empowered to self-organize and to work through a problem or an opportunity (perhaps through a series of sprints) to achieve a specific outcome, present it back, and then either continue or disband, as appropriate. These groups develop their own rhythm of work, have purposeful intent, and benefit from the diversity of their membership. For very little (if any) investment, the organization reaps huge rewards – both from the substance of what is produced and also the culture, behavior, and skills developed along the way. These initiatives also serve as opportunities for leaders to develop and practice their agile leadership habits and skills (as explored in **Chapter 6**) and for new leaders to emerge. The practice of "mastermind groups" and other peer-to-peer coaching and learning groups are growing in popularity and taking the more passive, traditional working groups and network models to a deeper level.

The future is complex and uncertain. Journeying and exploring that path with others who share a similar energy and general outlook helps to provide the resilience, support, and stretch of mindset needed to both validate and challenge our own assumptions. Those assumptions have the power to impact the options and issues we are solving for in shaping the next phase of work and working life.

Get the support you need

An exciting and liberating feature of the changing world of work – powered by global connectivity and enabling technology – is the emergence of individuals and organizations, both large and small, who can help you navigate the Future of Work. Historically, access to advice, expertise, and support was limited to the larger consulting firms or perhaps state sponsored bodies and institutes. Now there is a diverse network of talent locally and globally that can be accessed over a single LinkedIn connection or Zoom call!

What can I do about it now, in the short-term, when I still have so many other shorter-term priorities and demands to consider?

When I established WorkMatters, our operating model was developed on the idea of providing clients with a single access point to seasoned, independent and experienced experts in their respective fields, locally and international, all connected by a common mission of helping people to navigate the Future of Work. It has been a privilege to meet and work with so many talented Future of Work activists and specialists and for our clients to have options beyond traditional 20th century models of support and advice. Whether though our WorkMatters Academy, our suite of consulting services, or the many other sources of support from others in this field, the main point is that accessible and affordable help is out there. Whatever your industry or field of knowledge, there is a mentor, coach, or expert who can help you with your exact circumstances for where you are and where you want to go.

Source the right talent and let them figure it out

During a workshop on the Future of Work with a leadership team a few years back, the group I was working with seemed both excited but also somewhat daunted by the underlying business and work trends emerging at pace for them, and the sheer scale of the change facing their organization and workforce. They asked:

- Where to start?
- What can we do in the short term?
- What action could we take today that would have a meaningful impact?
- How do we set ourselves up for success?

The clear consensus on the first answer to these questions was talent. We explored ways in which they could literally start the next day to rethink how they recruited, developed, and promoted their leaders and their key talent for the future. It was clear that the criteria for selection and promotion had not really changed in over 20 years. The same patterns and biases existed in terms of what talent meant in the organization and what skills and attributes were *really* valued *versus* those they *claimed* were valued. Calling out these inconsistencies and resetting the criteria for what a Future of Work leader and employee actually meant for them – in terms of mindset and skillset – was perhaps the most important action this organization took toward a new strategy for the future.

Rethinking how they might access specialist skills through global networks of agency, platform and gig talent pools rather than depending on traditional employment methods and models was also another pattern and assumption regarding talent management that needed to be challenged.

With the right leaders, the right talent, and the right culture, there was confidence that the company could continue to adapt to the changes ahead. That confidence proved to be merited when COVID-19 hit a few years later, and the company outperformed its peers in its ability to pivot, perform, and change. As presented in **Chapter 2**, research from the likes of Joseph McCann and John Selsky bears this reality out over time, clearly demonstrating the difference that having agile talent at leadership, team, and individual levels made in how organizations thrived following major disruption and crisis *versus* those that didn't.

Adopt an agile mindset

Ultimately, the key take-away from this book is about shaping our own individual outlook on the future and being more deliberate about how we approach it. We have explored how having an agile mindset is a core and critical starting point whether you are an employee, a business leader, an HR professional, a policy-maker, politician, or citizen. With an agile mindset, we can adapt to whatever disruption is presented in the future, as inevitably it will.

The agile mindset and skillset explored in **Chapters 3** and **4** give us the personal, modern-day tools to go beyond reacting and/or responding to events as they unfold. These tools allow us to be open and to embrace challenge and continuous change through purposeful, empowered, forward-looking, and outcome-oriented action. They enable positive movement, learning and growth towards what we seek; not just an ability to react, cope and adapt to what work and working life throws at us. Let's keep the conversation going about how we can learn more about these adaptive qualities and skills, and how we can all help others around us to develop them and to thrive in their future working life. It will be interesting to look back in the years to come to see what kind of working world we individually and collectively chose to create for ourselves and for the next generation.

An abundant Future of Work is there if we want it, so perhaps, it is fitting to end where we began, with Charles Handy's words:

The future is not inevitable. We can influence it, if we know what we want it to be.

SELECTED FURTHER READING & REFERENCES

Chapter 1

Benko, C. & Donovan, J., AT&T's Talent Overhaul. *Harvard Business Review* (Online). Available: https://hbr.org/2016/10/atts-talent-overhaul.

Brynjolfsson, E. & McAfee, A. (2014). *The Second Machine Age*. New York/London: W.W Norton & Company.

Deloitte (2016). *Global Human Capital Trends 2016* [Online]. Available: https://www2.deloitte.com/content/dam/Deloitte/global/Documents /HumanCapital/gx-dup-global-human-capital-trends-2016.pdf (Accessed: April 14, 2017).

Ford, M. (2015). *Rise of the Robots: Technology & the Threat of a Jobless Future*. New York: Basic Books.

Handy, C. (1995). *The Age of Unreason*. 2nd Ed. London: Arrow Books Ltd.

Kotter, J.P. (2012). Accelerate!, *Harvard Business Review*, 90(11), pp.44-58.

McGrath, R. (2013). *The End of Competitive Advantage*. Boston: Harvard Business School Publishing.

Schwab, K. (2016). *The Fourth Industrial Revolution*. Geneva: World Economic Forum.

The Gig Economy Data Hub [Online]. Available: https://www.gigeconomydata.org/research.

Chapter 2

.Glenn, M. (2009). *Organizational Agility: How Business can Survive & Thrive in Turbulent Times.* London: Economist Intelligence Unit.

Holbeche, L. (2015). *The Agile Organization.* London/Philadelphia/New Delhi: Kogan Page Ltd.

McCann, J. & Selsky, J. (2012) *Mastering Turbulence: The Essential Capabilities of Agile and Resilient Individuals, Teams and Organizations.* Hoboken, NJ: John Wiley & Sons.

McKinsey (2017). *Global Survey: Organizational Agility* [Online]. Available: https://www.mckinsey.com/business-functions/organization/our-insights/how-to-create-an-agile-organization.

Muduli, A. (2016). Exploring the facilitators and mediators of workforce agility: An empirical study, *Management Research Review*, Vol.39(12), p.1570.

Weill, P. (2006). *MIT CIO Summit.* MIT Sloan School of Management's Center for Information Systems Research.

Yang, C. & Liu, H. (2012). Boosting firm performance *via* enterprise agility & network structure, *Management Decision*, 50(6), pp.1022-44.

Chapter 3

David, S. (2016). *Emotional Agility.* Penguin Random House.

Denning, S. (2015). Agile: It's time to put it to use to manage business complexity, *Strategy & Leadership*, (2015), pp.10-17.

Dweck, C.S. (2012). *Mindset: How You Can Fulfil Your Potential.* New York: Random House.

Johnson, G., Whittington, R. & Scholes, K. (2011). *Exploring Strategy, Text & Cases.* Harlow, Essex: Pearson Education Ltd.

Ulrich, D., Kryscynski, D., Brockbank, W. & Ulrich, M. (2017). *Victory through Organization: Why the War for Talent is Failing Your Company and What You Can Do about It.* New York: McGraw-Hill.

Chapter 4

Carlisi, C., Hemerling, J., Kilmann, J., Meese, D. & Shipman, D. (2017). Purpose with the power to transform your organization (Online).

Available: https://www.bcg.com/publications/2017/ transformation-behavior-culture-purpose-power-transform-organization.aspx (Accessed: June 30, 2018).

Cross, R., Martin, R. & Weiss, L. (2006). Mapping the value of employee collaboration (Online). Available: https://www.mckinsey.com/business-functions/organization/our-insights/mapping-the-value-of-employee-collaboration (Accessed: July 1, 2018).

Empey, K.J. (2019). *Personal Agility: The New Skills Set for the Changing World of Work*. (Online). Available: www.workmatters.ie.

McCann, J. & Selsky, J.W. (2012). Being purposeful in turbulent environments, *People & Strategy*, 35(4), pp.28-34.

Senge, P.M. (1990). *The Fifth Discipline*. London: Random House.

Sherehiy, B., Karwowski, W. & Layer, J.K. (2007). A review of enterprise agility: Concepts, frameworks, and attributes, *International Journal of Industrial Ergonomics*, 37(2007), pp.445-460.

Ulrich, D., Kryscynski, D., Brockbank, W. & Ulrich, M. (2017). *Victory through Organization: Why the War for Talent is Failing Your Company and What You Can Do about It*. New York: McGraw-Hill.

Chapter 5

Meister, J.C. & Mulcahy, K.J. (2017). The Future Workplace Experience. New York: McGraw-Hill.

Meister, J.C. & Willyerd, K. (2010). *The 2020 Workplace*. New York: HarperCollins.

Moss Kanter, R. (2001) *Evolve: Succeeding in the Digital Culture of Tomorrow*. Boston: Harvard Business School Press.

Chapter 6

Fisk, P. (2002). The making of a digital leader, *Business Strategy Review*, 13(1), pp.43-50.

Goffee, R. & Jones, G. (2006). *Why Should Anyone Be Led By You*. Boston: Harvard Business School Press.

Hesselbein, F., Goldsmith, M. & Beckhard, R. (1997). *The Organization of the Future*. San Francisco: Jossey-Bass.

Joiner, B. & Josephs, S. (2007). *Leadership Agility.* San Francisco: Jossey-Bass.

Lurie, M. (2015). The Age of Agile Leadership, *Chief Learning Officer,* 14(7), pp.26-33.

Schein, E.H. (1999). *The Corporate Culture Survival Guide.* San Francisco: Jossey-Bass Inc.

Chapter 7

McMackin, J. & Heffernan, M. (2020). Agile for HR: Fine in practice, but will it work in theory? *Human Resource Management Review* (Online). Available: https://www.sciencedirect.com/science/article/pii/S1053482220300644 (Accessed: October 15, 2020).

Taylor, M. (2017). *Good Work: The Taylor Review of Modern Working Practices.* London: HMSO.

Thorén, P.M. (2017). *Agile People: A Radical Approach for HR and Managers.* Carson City, NV: Lioncrest Publishing.

Chapter 8

Laloux, F. (2014). *Reinventing Organizations: A Guide to Creating Organizations Inspired by the Next Stage in Human Consciousness.* Millis, MA: Parker Nelson.

Chapter 9

Handy, C. (1995). *The Age of Unreason.* 2nd Ed. London: Arrow Books Ltd.

Ulrich, D. & Ulrich, W. (2010). *The Why of Work,* New York: McGraw Hill.

ABOUT THE AUTHOR

KEVIN EMPEY has specialized in organization development, leadership development and people strategy for over 25 years.

With a background originally in technology and business development, Kevin developed an international career in people consulting and leadership development, working across a wide range of organizations, sectors and geographies. Before establishing WorkMatters, a training and consulting firm specializing in the changing world of work, he was a Partner and Director in Willis Towers Watson, where he led the firm's HR consulting business in Ireland.

Kevin is an associate leadership development faculty member with the Irish Management Institute and is Program Director of its flagship Senior Executive Program. He is a Chartered Fellow of the CIPD and served on the Top-Level Appointments Committee (TLAC), which advises on the selection of senior civil service appointments in Ireland. A leading expert on the Future of Work, Kevin was also a member of the Labor Market Council in Ireland and was the founder of Worklink, an internationally recognized coaching and mentoring organization set up to help unemployed jobseekers into full-time employment. Kevin has won several national and international awards for his work in the areas of employment policy, social entrepreneurship, and Future of Work research.

INDEX